CULTURES OF THE WORLD

Estonia

Michael Spilling

mc Marshall Cavendish
Benchmark
New York

PICTURE CREDITS

Cover: © Image Source/Getty Images
A.N.A. Press Agency: 120, 121 • altTYPE/REUTERS: 31 • altTYPE/REUTERS/Ints Kalnin: 33, 35 • altTYPE/ REUTERS/Nikola Solic: 34 • Art Directors & Trip: 26, 37, 67, 114 • Bes Stock: 24, 28, 47, 48, 52, 53, 80, 91, 95, 96, 126, 127, 128, 129, 130, 131 • Corbis Inc.: 8, 18, 46, 99, 103, 122 • Eye Ubiquitous: 97 • Getty Images : 16, 64, 65, 66, 69, 70 73, 75, 77, 90, 92, 93, 101, 102, 109, 116 • Hutchison Library: 85, 86 • Lonely Planet Images: 42, 79, 82 • National Geographic Images: 54 • Photolibrary: 1, 3, 5, 6, 7, 9, 10, 11, 12, 13, 14, 15, 17, 19, 20, 21, 22, 23, 30, 40, 43, 44, 45, 50, 51, 55, 56, 57, 58, 59, 60, 61, 62, 63, 68, 72, 74, 76, 78, 83, 84, 87, 88, 89, 98, 100, 104, 106, 107, 108, 110, 111, 112, 113, 115, 117, 123, 124, 125

PRECEDING PAGE
Estonians in their traditional outfits stand in front of the Schwarzhaeupterhaus in Tallinn.

Publisher (U.S.): Michelle Bisson
Editors: Deborah Grahame, Mindy Pang
Copyreader: Sherry Chiger
Designers: Nancy Sabato, Benson Tan
Cover picture researcher: Connie Gardner
Picture researcher: Thomas Khoo

Marshall Cavendish Benchmark
99 White Plains Road
Tarrytown, NY 10591
Website: www.marshallcavendish.us

© Times Media Private Limited 1999
© Marshall Cavendish International (Asia) Private Limited 2010
® "Cultures of the World" is a registered trademark of Times Publishing Limited.

Originated and designed by Times Media Private Limited
An imprint of Marshall Cavendish International (Asia) Private Limited
A member of Times Publishing Limited

Marshall Cavendish is a trademark of Times Publishing Limited.

Library of Congress Cataloging-in-Publication Data
Spilling, Michael.
  Estonia / by Michael Spilling. -- 2nd ed.
      p. cm. -- (Cultures of the world)
  Includes bibliographical references and index.
  Summary: "Provides comprehensive information on the geography, history,
    wildlife, governmental structure, economy, cultural diversity, peoples,
    religion, and culture of Estonia"--Provided by publisher.
  ISBN 978-0-7614-4846-4
  1. Estonia--Juvenile literature. I. Title.
  DK503.23.S65 2010
  947.98--dc22   2009021201

Printed in China
7 6 5 4 3 2 1

CONTENTS

INTRODUCTION

WASHED BY THE THE BALTIC SEA, Estonia is a small, newly independent country in the northeast of the Baltic region. Invaded and occupied successively by the Germans, the Danes, the Swedes, the Poles, and the Russians, Estonia has developed a rich cultural heritage that combines traditions from Scandinavia, the Baltic German trading cities, and the former Soviet Union. Since gaining independence from the Soviet Union in 1991, Estonia has been one of the great success stories of Eastern Europe, transforming itself into a high-tech, forward-looking country with a vibrant culture, a dynamic economy, and a stable democracy despite its small size and limited resources. Estonia has quickly built ties with Western Europe, becoming a member of both the European Union (EU) and the North Atlantic Treaty Organization (NATO) in 2004. Estonia today has more in common with modern, wealthy Scandinavia than with its fellow former Soviet republics in Eastern Europe.

GEOGRAPHY

Autumn view of the Haanja Landscape Reserve in southern Estonia.

CHAPTER 1

The fields of northern Estonia are littered with great boulders—remnants of glacial activity from the Ice Age.

SITUATED ON THE EASTERN SHORE OF the Baltic Sea, the Republic of Estonia —or Eesti Vabariik, as it is called in Estonian—is the most northerly and least populated of the three Baltic states (Estonia, Latvia, Lithuania). This small former Soviet republic is 17,462 square miles (45,226 square km) in area—about half the size of Maine, but with the same population.

Estonia's long coastline is washed by the Baltic Sea on the west and the Gulf of Finland on the north. Latvia is to the south, while the Narva River and Lake Peipsi divide Estonia from its large and powerful Russian neighbor in the east. Much of Estonia borders the sea; including the islands, Estonia has 2,357 miles (3,794 km) of highly indented coastline. For most Estonians, the natural beauty of the thinly populated western coast and islands epitomizes all that is good about their country, and they consider this area the very essence of Estonian life and culture. Although geographically part of Eastern Europe, Estonia—unlike Latvia and Lithuania—is more Nordic in character, a Scandinavian land stranded on the wrong side of the Baltic Sea. Tallinn, Estonia's capital, is just a 53-mile (85-km) boat ride from Helsinki, the capital of Finland.

Estonia is famous for its large deposits of limestone. The walls of the Dominican monastery at Saint Catherine's Alley in Tallinn were constructed of limestone.

THE LAND

Estonia can be divided into two distinct geographic areas: a coastal region in the north and west characterized by low-lying marshes, lakes, and islands, and a plain in the east and south that is higher in elevation, typically 161 feet (49 m) above sea level.

Just 10 percent of the land area lies more than 299 feet (91 m) above sea level. Suur Munamägi (Large Egg Hill) is Estonia's highest point at 1,040 feet (317 m) and is in fact the highest point in the Baltic region.

The plain in the south is situated on the northern edge of the North European Plain, a vast, flat landscape that stretches westward from northern Germany through Poland, the Baltic countries, and northern Russia. The higher part of the plain runs north to south through the eastern part of Estonia and includes the Pandivere Plateau, the Otepää Plateau, and the Haanja Plateau. Southern and eastern Estonia are predominantly rural in character.

A windmill in the village of Jamajala on the island of Saaremaa. Windmills still dot the countryside, reminders of the hundreds that were once used to power Estonia.

The low-lying areas in the west and north include the whole coastal area and have extensive marshlands, more than 1,400 lakes, and more than 1,500 islands. The northern coast, around the cities of Tallinn, Kohtla-Järve, and Narva, is home to most of Estonia's industry.

REGIONS

Estonia is divided into 15 *maakonnad* (MAH-kon-ahd), or counties. Harjumaa, in the north, is the country's most populous *maakond* (MAH-kont) and includes the capital, Tallinn. In the northeast are the two counties of Lääne-Virumaa and Ida-Virumaa. The three counties of Järvamaa, Jõgevamaa, and Viljandimaa occupy the center of Estonia. In the south, the *maakond*

Fresh snow on a lake in an Estonian forest in January.

of Tartumaa includes the ancient city of Tartu. The other three counties in the south are Põlvamaa, Võrumaa, and Valgamaa. In the west, the *maakond* of Pärnumaa includes the historic city of Pärnu. Läänemaa covers the northwest coastal area of Estonia. The county of Raplamaa includes the administrative town of Rapla. The island of Saaremaa is part of a *maakond* that includes the island of Muhu and 500 smaller islands. The island of Hiiumaa is also a *maakond*.

CLIMATE AND SEASONS

Estonia has a temperate and sometimes humid climate. Winters are milder than in corresponding latitudes because cold air masses are warmed by passage over the Gulf Stream and the Baltic Sea. Consequently warm air hits Estonia in winter and cool air in summer. In general the northern and western coastal areas have a milder climate than the higher, inland region. The inland areas in the south and east experience a more extreme continental climate, with hot summers and cold winters. Winter arrives in November and does not end until March or sometimes April. Spring and fall are generally cold and wet.

LAKES AND RIVERS

Lakes are one of the country's most characteristic features. There are about 1,450 natural and man-made lakes, whose water area exceeds 2.5 acres (1 ha). Lakes cover 6.1 percent of Estonia and are unevenly distributed over the territory. Most of the lakes are shallow; just 20 or so are deeper than 66 feet (20 m). Lake Rõuge Suurjärv is the deepest at 125 feet (38 m).

Lake Peipsi, with an area of 1,350 square miles (3,496 square km), is the fourth largest lake in Europe and is considered one of the best fishing spots; it is home to more than 30 species of fish. Today it provides Estonia with 90 percent of its inland fishing production. Estonia's second largest lake, Võrtsjärv (104 square miles/269 square km), is just west of the Otepää Plateau. The lake is used mainly for fishing and as a reservoir.

Numerous rivers flow across Estonia's sandstone and limestone plains. The Väike-Emajõgi River springs from the Otepää highlands and flows into Lake Võrtsjärv; it emerges as the Emajõgi (meaning "Mother River") to the north and winds its way eastward through Tartumaa, eventually flowing into Lake Peipsi. At 130 miles (209 km), it is Estonia's longest river. The Pärnu River is 89 miles (143 km) long, while to the north, the Narva River (49 miles/79 km) links Lake Peipsi to the Gulf of Finland. Other major rivers include the Põltsamaa, the Võhandu, the Kasari, and the Pirita.

Submerged stones on the coast of Lake Peipsi.

Estonia is famous for its beautiful springs, of which there are thousands. The largest of them are Roosna-Alliku, Esna, Prandi, Varangu, and Simuna, which are located in and around the Pandivere Upland. The water in the lakes that have underwater springs is transparent and cold. Many springs are located in villages or near farms and manor houses; this is because in the past, Estonians would build their homes near the springs so that they would have a permanent and clean water supply.

FLORA AND FAUNA

There are about 18,000 species of wildlife in Estonia, of which more than half are insects. Among the 90 species of trees and shrubs, the most common tree is pine, followed by birch, aspen, and fir. Less numerous though still common trees include oak, alder, and spruce.

Beautiful blue and purple cornflowers grow in the wild woodlands of Estonia.

About 65 species of mammals live in Estonia, mainly woodland and forest creatures. The magnificent elk and other deer, wild boars, badgers, foxes, squirrels, and beavers are common inhabitants, while the rarer brown bears, wolves, and lynx can still be seen.

With its long, indented coastline, many islands, reedbeds, wetlands, and marshes, Estonia is an ideal nesting ground for both local and migratory birds. There are 329 species of birds identified in Estonia. Of these, 222 species breed in the country, 38 are transitory migrants or winter visitors—such as migrating geese, swans, ducks, and storks—and the rest are occasional visitors. Of the year-round residents, the most common are sparrows, blackbirds, woodcocks, and golden eagles. Estonia's national bird is the graceful barn swallow.

The black-and-white barn swallow is the national bird of Estonia, and its colors, along with the blue of the cornflower, make up the colors of the Estonian flag.

An aerial view of Tallinn Old Town.

CITIES

As a predominantly rural country, Estonia has no cities of any great size. Nevertheless the capital, Tallinn (population 403,547), is one of the most beautiful and picturesque cities in the Baltic region. Its streets seem to tumble down the side of a fortress-topped hill, Toompea, and spread out into Tallinn Bay. Originally established by Danish conquerors in the 13th century, Tallinn (meaning "Danish fortress") still has a strongly medieval character with cobbled sidewalks, walls, and numerous towers, turrets, and spires.

Tallinn has always been strategically important in the eastern Baltic and consequently has been occupied by Denmark, Sweden, and Russia in the course of its history. This has given the city a special, cosmopolitan atmosphere. However, the dominant influence is German, and much of the city has a strong medieval German flavor.

The Old Town area of Tallinn was named a UNESCO World Heritage site in 1997 for its well-preserved medieval architecture and cobbled streets.

Many of the Hanseatic towers that were a part of the city's fortifications have been preserved, Pikk Hermann (Tall Hermann) being one of the most notable. *Toompea*—the name of the fortress and the old town on the crest of the hill—derives from the German word *domberg*, which means "cathedral mountain."

Estonia's second-largest city, Tartu (population 105,000), is in the southeast of the country on the Emajõgi. Tartu was built as a stronghold in the 11th century by the Grand Duke of Kiev. Much of the old town has been destroyed in wars throughout Estonia's turbulent history, and most of its existing buildings date from the 18th century. A university was established in Tartu in 1632, and ever since, the city has been considered the spiritual and cultural center of Estonia. Tartu was the center of the nationalist and cultural revival in the 19th century, with the first National Song Festival held there in 1869.

The famous kissing sculpture and fountain in the Town Hall Square of Tartu.

Located in the industrial northeast of Estonia on the Russian border, Narva (population 67,000) is Estonia's third-largest city. It is separated from the Russian city of Ivangorod by the Narva River and is populated almost entirely by ethnic Russians. Narva is closer to Russia's traditional northern capital, Saint Petersburg, than it is to Tallinn. Narva's heavy industries are a stark contrast to Estonia's predominantly rural character. Narva was a German trading town as far back as the 12th century. The city was almost completely destroyed in World War II, and little of the historic town remains.

Kohtla-Järve (population 46,000), Estonia's fourth-largest city, is 30 miles (48 km) west of Narva. It is a modern industrial city built 60 years ago as a result of oil-shale mining in the area. Pärnu (population 44,000) is Estonia's fifth-largest city and is located on the Gulf of Riga. The town developed around a German fort built in the 13th century. It is Estonia's leading seaside resort and health spa.

ISLAND RETREATS

Estonia's islands, which constitute as much as 10 percent of the country's total territory, contain perhaps the most unspoiled and most secluded landscapes in the country. Only two islands are of any significant size: Saaremaa (1,030 square miles/2,668 square km) and Hiiumaa (382 square miles/989 square km). Saaremaa has a population of 40,000, while Hiiumaa is inhabited by 12,000 people. Clustered off the western shore of the mainland, the islands have maintained a traditional, quiet, and distinctly Estonian way of life. Before 1991 the Soviet authorities helped maintain the islands' natural state. The islands were thought to be escape routes to the West because of their seclusion, so while some parts of Estonia were polluted by Soviet industrial projects, the islands were not developed. Military personnel were the only visitors allowed on the islands for many years.

Saaremaa is a scenic island with many charming fishing villages, neat cottages, nature reserves, beach resorts, windmills, and pine forests. On the northern edge of the island there are picturesque limestone formations. From here, the Panga Scarp, the island's highest cliff at 72 feet (22 m), offers a superb view of the clear, green Baltic Sea. The island includes a strange and unique phenomenon: the massive Kaali Crater (below), formed by a 1,000-ton (907-metric-ton) meteorite in the eighth century B.C. It is one of the most accessible meteorite craters in the world.

Because it is filled with opaque green water, some people think it resembles a large bowl of pea soup! The capital of Saaremaa, Kuressaare (population 15,000), has a well-preserved 14th-century castle. To reach Saaremaa from the mainland, it is necessary to take a ferry to the smaller, neighboring island of Muhu. The causeway that links Muhu and Saaremaa is one of the most beautiful spots in Estonia, with the water colored green with swaying reeds. In the spring thousands of swans go there to mate. Muhu is Estonia's third-largest island and has a population of just 1,800.

Hiiumaa includes numerous stately homes and some remarkable lighthouses. The Kõpu Lighthouse (right) was first lit in 1531 and is thought to be the third-oldest continuously operating lighthouse in the world. The capital of Hiiumaa, Kärdla, is a small town of some 4,000 people. There is now a small airport at Kärdla offering local flights to Tallinn. Very few people live in the heart of the island, where there are peat bogs and swamps. Hiiumaa is rich in flora and boasts more than 900 species of plants, including rare orchids. Many of Estonia's artists have summerhouses on Hiiumaa. The most popular spot for summer cottages, however, is Kassari, the largest of 400 islands that hug the southern coast of Hiiumaa. Junipers are Kassari's most common plant. They are used in every way imaginable: the wood for butter knives to stop the butter turning rancid; the branches for sauna switches; the berries as a vodka spice.

HISTORY

Built by the Danes in the 1370s, this castle on the bank of the Narva River was continually improved by the Swedish and Russian rulers.

CHAPTER 2

ESTONIANS HAVE EXISTED AS A people since ancient times. Despite this long-acknowledged identity, they have rarely been masters of their own domain. Because Estonia is one of the smallest and least populated countries in Europe, its history has been one of domination by outsiders. Sweden, Denmark, Poland, Russia, and most significantly, Germany have left strong impressions.

Estonia enjoyed its first, short-lived period of independence from 1918 to 1940. Those years were a source of inspiration to future generations of Estonians and provided them with the motivation to grasp their freedom when the Soviet empire crumbled in the late 1980s.

BEGINNINGS

Estonians were first described at length by the Roman historian Tacitus in *Germania*, referring to them as Aestii: "In producing of grain and the other fruits of the earth, they labor with more assiduity and patience than is suitable to the usual laziness of Germans. Nay, they even search the deep, and of all the rest are the only people

Throughout the Soviet occupation of Estonia, the United States government never recognized the legitimacy of Soviet rule and continued to deal with the Estonian Consulate in New York as the legal representative of Estonia.

Fortified villages, like this one in Tallinn, were built for defense.

The crusaders attacking a castle during their great conquest.

who gather amber. They call it glesum, and find it amongst the shallows and upon the very shore." In the fifth century A.D. Slavic tribes appeared southeast of present-day Estonia. Estonians then built fortified villages to defend themselves.

In the ninth century, Estonia was a part of the Viking trade route from Scandinavia to the Slavic countries, Byzantium, and the Caspian Sea. Around this time, agricultural improvements were made: Households owned cultivated land, while forest and other land surrounding a village was commonly shared by the villagers.

CRUSADER CONQUEST

In the 11th and 12th centuries, the Slavs made many incursions into Estonia but failed to establish supremacy. The Danes and the Swedes also made unsuccessful attempts to Christianize the Estonians. German monks began preaching Christianity along the Baltic coast in 1180 but met with little success.

In 1193 the pope in Rome declared a northern crusade in an attempt to convert the Baltic peoples to Christianity, and the first Livonian Crusade was launched in the Baltic region in 1198. German merchants, who were eager to open up the Baltic region to German trade, supported the pope's proclamation. Under the leadership of Albert von Buxhoevden, German knights responded to the pope's call by forming the Brothers of the Sword and mounting a military invasion of the Baltic coast in 1200. They wore the famous crusader capes with a black cross on a white background. The knights soon established the city of Riga in 1201. By 1208 they had subdued the Livs and Latgalians, tribes to the south of Estonia, and set up many important trading outposts along the Baltic coast.

From 1208 onward, the German knights turned their attention to Estonia. The Estonians lost men steadily, while the knights constantly replenished their forces with fresh crusaders from Germany. The Estonian military leader, Lembitu, organized a fierce resistance, but he was killed in 1217. Estonia's lack of a centralized command or power structure made it difficult for Estonians to unite and resist invasion. Tribes and clans were conquered in turn and forcibly baptized by the fierce crusaders. Most of southern Estonia was subdued by 1218. Northern Estonia was not conquered until 1219, when Albert's ally, the crusading King Valdemar II of Denmark, captured the site of Tallinn and founded the city. By 1220 all of Estonia except the island of Saaremaa was under German and Danish control. The island was finally subdued by the knights in the winter of 1227 when the Baltic froze and they were able to mount an assault with ease.

Alexander Nevsky, the legendary hero who defeated the knights of the Teutonic Order.

GERMAN RULE

In 1237 the Brothers of the Sword were beaten in battle by the Lithuanians, and the remnants were joined to the much stronger Germany-based Teutonic Order, one of the largest and most powerful crusading organizations in Europe. The crusaders' attempt to expand east was brought to an end by the Russians in 1242 at the famous Battle of the Ice on Lake Peipsi when the legendary Alexander Nevsky (1220—63) decisively defeated the knights.

Martin Luther,
German Protestant
reformer and
founder of
the Lutheran
movement.

The area known as Livonia came under the control of the Teutonic Order. Northern Estonia was ruled by the Danes. The Teutonic Order absorbed Estonia into the Hanseatic League, a loose trading association of German towns and states along the Baltic coast. Estonia's economy was soon transformed into one of the best farming and trading communities of the Middle Ages.

In 1343 the Estonian peasantry rose up against their foreign masters, determined to end their subjugation. Tallinn was besieged, and many Germans were killed on the islands of Saaremaa and Hiiumaa. Thousands of Estonians were slaughtered in revenge, and no further uprisings were attempted for 200 years. In 1346 Denmark, whose power had been waning, sold northern Estonia to the Livonian Order, a branch of the Teutonic Order.

The Germans dominated Baltic culture for the next two centuries. German merchants controlled commerce and the town councils, and German clergy administered the churches, while German nobles owned most of the land. The Estonians and Latvians—who made up 95 percent of the population—became serfs owned by the German nobles.

END OF THE TEUTONIC ORDER

At the end of the 15th century, three new powers emerged around the borders of Livonia: Poland—Lithuania, a united kingdom to the south; Sweden; and Muscovite Russia. Territorial disputes led to wars between Poland and the Teutonic Order in 1454 and 1519.

In 1519 the head of the Livonian Order, Grand Master Albert, met the great Christian reformer Martin Luther (1483—1546). Luther advised Albert to secularize his vast estates and stop paying any more taxes to Rome. In 1524 Tallinn's synod adopted Luther's First Principles of the Reformation, and the other towns in Estonia soon followed. Henceforth, Estonia was a Protestant country. The ordinary Estonians, however, remained largely indifferent to these changes, since the majority of the clergy were German.

The destruction of Rome's influence led to the breakup and eventual dissolution of the Teutonic and Livonian orders in 1561. The Livonian Wars plunged the country into 25 years of turmoil. The Russians, under Ivan the Terrible (1530—84), penetrated deep into Estonian territory in 1558, devastating the area and weakening the military power of the Livonian Order. In the 1560s, the German nobility in northerm Estonia turned to Sweden for protection, while southern Estonia submitted to Poland.

In 1584 Sweden—having expelled the Russians—emerged as the dominant power in northern Estonia, while Poland maintained control of southern Estonia. In 1599 wars of succession led to further wars between Sweden and Poland—Lithuania. Estonia was again ravaged by foreign armies, and the Estonian population suffered heavy casualties from war, disease, and famine. In 1629, as part of the Truce of Altmark, Poland—Lithuania surrendered southern Estonia to Sweden, leaving the Scandinavians the dominant power in the Baltic.

Ivan the Terrible, leader of the Russians.

The chronicler Christian Kelch wrote in 1695, "Estonia is the landlord's heaven, the clergy's paradise, the stranger's gold mine, and the peasant's hell."

SWEDISH INFLUENCE

Following the Truce of Altmark, the Swedish empire encompassed much of the Baltic region, including Estonia, Livonia, Finland, Western Pomerania, and Bremen. Many of the German-descended Baltic barons were given land by the Swedish king Gustavus Adolphus (1594—1632) in an attempt to win their loyalty. Unfortunately the German landlords abused their position by increasing taxes and extorting excessive unpaid labor from the peasants. Isolated rebellions broke out but were not successful.

THE GREAT NORTHERN WAR (1700-21)

In 1697 the 15-year-old Charles XII (1682—1718, pictured left) was crowned king of Sweden. Russia, Denmark, and Poland judged that the time was ripe to end Swedish domination of the Baltic region and formed an alliance in 1699. A titanic struggle ensued between Charles and Peter the Great of Russia. In November 1700 a Russian force of 35,000 men led by Peter marched on Narva, which was held by a small Swedish garrison. Charles hurried to the town's aid and plunged his newly arrived army of 8,000 men into battle. The poorly equipped and badly trained Russians were taken by surprise, and Peter lost every piece of artillery he possessed. However, instead of pursuing his advantage and pressing on to Moscow, Charles turned his attention to Poland.

With Charles's army in Poland, Peter reinvaded the Baltic region and captured Narva and Tartu in 1704. In 1708 every major building in Tartu was destroyed: According to an old saying, "No dog barked and no rooster crowed from Tartu to Narva."

In 1708 Charles renewed his campaign against Russia through Ukraine. However, at the Battle of Poltava (1709), Charles's army was destroyed by the Russians. During the next 10 years Sweden's Baltic possessions were seized by Denmark, Prussia, and Russia. Having gained Finland in 1714, Peter launched an invasion of Sweden in 1719. At the Peace of Nystad in 1721, Sweden was forced to concede all the Baltic provinces to Russia, and Estonia came under Russian control.

The Swedish king Charles XI (1655—97) later attempted to curb the power of the landlords. Baltic barons who could not prove landownership by presenting title deeds were made tenants of the crown or replaced by Swedish landlords.

Under the Swedes, education was introduced at the parish level, and in the 1630s the first books in Estonian appeared. Printing shops were opened in Tartu and Tallinn. Gustavus Adolphus established a university at Tartu in 1632, and by 1688 there were more than 1,000 students in schools throughout Estonia and Livonia.

CZARIST RULE

Swedish influence ended in the eastern Baltic following the Great Northern War (1700—21). Peter I (1672—1725), called Peter the Great, defeated Sweden and expanded Russia's border to the Baltic Sea. Peter had built the city of Saint Petersburg at the mouth of the Neva River in 1703, providing Russia with a permanent outlet to the Baltic Sea and a future northern capital.

Initially Russian rule meant few changes for the Estonians. Similar to the Swedes before him, Peter sought to win over the German landlords by giving them more power. The landlords, who constituted only 1 percent of the population, controlled the administration, as well

Czar Alexander II.

as owned all the land. In 1739 the Rosen Declaration—written by Baron von Rosen, chairman of the Livonian diet, or assembly—formalized the practices of centuries-old serfdom. Landlords were legally entitled to buy and sell peasants as they pleased, decide marriages, and administer corporal punishment. Later, under Czarina Catherine II (1729—96), peasants were also selected by lottery to serve as conscripts in the Russian army. During a visit to the Baltic provinces in 1764, Czarina Catherine II was distressed at the appalling conditions of the serfs and recommended reforms. However, the German landlords ignored most of her suggestions. Peasant unrest in 1805, 1817, 1820, and 1858 had little effect. In 1801 Czar Alexander I (1777—1825) appointed a governor-general to administer the Baltic region. Diets were set up in mainland Estonia, Livonia, and Saaremaa and were run by 12 councillors who were elected for life.

Czar Alexander III of Russia and Czarina Maria Feodorovna.

Conditions did improve for the peasants following the abolition of serfdom in Estonia in 1816, although it was not abolished across the wider Russian empire until 1861 by Czar Alexander II (1818—81). Peasants were allowed to pay money to rent their land, rather than paying rent in kind (usually labor). They were free to conduct their own business and could choose their own marriage partners without asking the landlord's permission. The barons were no longer allowed to buy and sell peasants or to use corporal punishment. Nevertheless, the best land remained in the possession of the landlords, and peasants were still required to serve in the army and pay a heavy poll tax. Although they had gained their personal freedom, the peasants continued to be oppressed by economic hardships.

In the 19th century Estonia began to develop an industrial base, mainly factories manufacturing paper, glass, and textiles. The urban population rapidly increased, and by the 1860s, ethnic Estonians were the majority in all urban centers for the first time. Czar Alexander III (1845—94) increased the Russification of the Baltic region, and Russian administrators replaced the Baltic Germans in the judiciary and the police force. Misdemeanors were harshly punished by the censorial Czarist police. Russian Orthodox churches were built in prominent central squares as part of this campaign in the 1880s and 1890s.

NATIONAL AWAKENING

In the latter half of the 19th century, social reforms, the growth of manufacturing, and increased prosperity led to a growing sense of national consciousness among urban Estonians. Estonian-language newspapers were first established in the 1850s, attempts were made to establish an Estonian-language high school, and a genuine Estonian intelligentsia developed. Radical

CONSCRIPTION

In Czarist Russia, military conscription was dreaded by the peasants, who could be sent to the far-flung reaches of the Russian empire to fight wars and suffer hardship and disease. The British author Lady Elizabeth Eastlake describes the situation in her 1841 travel memoir, A Residence on the Shores of the Baltic: *"From the moment that the peasant of the Baltic provinces draws the fatal lot no. 1, he knows that he is a Russian, and, worse than that, a Russian soldier, and not only himself, but every son from that hour born to him; like the executioner's office in Germany, a soldier's life is hereditary... If wars and climate and sickness and hardship spare him, he returns after four-and-twenty years of service—his language scarce remembered, his religion changed, and with not a ruble in his pocket—to seek his daily bread by his own exertions for the remainder of his life, or to be chargeable to his parish, who by this time have forgotten that he ever existed, and certainly wish he had never returned."*

left-wing politics made an impact in all parts of imperial Russia for much of the latter half of the 19th century. At the All-Estonian Congress in Tartu in November 1905, both liberals and radicals demanded Estonian autonomy and a halt to Russification. The Czarist authorities declared martial law to suppress the fledgling political movement, and workers scattered to the countryside and began looting and burning the country manors. As a consequence, troops were sent to Estonia, and many revolutionaries were arrested and sentenced to death.

INDEPENDENCE WON

The outbreak of World War I in 1914 did not have much effect on Estonia. However, German war goals included occupying the eastern edge of the Baltic and turning it into an area for future German settlement. Many of the German barons in the Baltic secretly supported this aim and viewed with alarm the growing aspirations of the Baltic people. Most Estonians supported the Russian fight against the imperialistic Germans, and 100,000 Estonians were drafted into the Russian army.

Tens of thousands of Estonians fought in the German army against the Soviet Union in World War II. Soviet authorities viewed this as collaboration, and Estonia's war record has been a source of tension with Russia ever since.

A monument to the heroes of the War of Independence.

In 1917 the debilitating effects of a disastrous war, food shortages, and a weak government led to social unrest throughout Czarist Russia. The Czarist government quickly collapsed, and a new provisional government under the leadership of Alexander Kerensky came to power. Workers' movements sprang up, and power was effectively split between the government and the workers.

On March 26, 1917, Estonian workers demonstrated in nearby Petrograd, as Saint Petersburg was now called. In response, the Kerensky government provisionally decreed home rule for Estonia. An Estonian national council, called the Maapäev, was established, and a provisional government was set up with Konstantin Päts (1874—1956) as president.

In November the Bolsheviks, under the leadership of Vladimir Lenin and Leon Trotsky, stormed the Winter Palace in Petrograd, igniting the first sparks of the Russian Revolution. The Bolsheviks also took control of Tallinn and established a puppet government. Within two months, however, German forces had advanced as far as Tallinn, routing the Communists. On February 24, 1918, the now-underground Maapäev declared Estonian independence. The next day, German forces occupied the city, arrested many Estonian leaders, and claimed sovereignty over the Baltic states. Päts was arrested too but set free in November, when Germany was defeated by the Allies. When World War I ended in November 1918, the retreating Germans left a gaping power vacuum. Päts and the independence movement again proclaimed Estonian independence, and the Bolshevik army promptly invaded Estonia. The Estonians received military assistance from Britain, Finland, Sweden, and Denmark, all of which supported Estonian calls for independence. The Estonian general Johannes Laidoner (1884—1953) led the Estonian army on a counteroffensive in January 1919. By the summer of 1919, the Estonians had been so successful that they had advanced to the edge of Riga in Latvia. Estonia had finally secured its borders and was an independent state for the first time in its history.

Elections had already been held, in April 1919, and Estonia's first Constituent Assembly was formed, with August Rei (1886—1963) as president. A coalition of socialists and liberals was represented in the assembly. A constitution was adopted in June 1920, and in 1921 Estonia gained international recognition and was admitted to the League of Nations. In 1924 the Communists attempted a coup in Tallinn but failed miserably. The Communist Party was thereafter outlawed in Estonia. In 1934, following serious political unrest in part caused by the world economic crisis, Päts disbanded parliament and engineered an authoritarian coup. Parliamentary elections were resumed in 1938, in which year Päts was declared president.

INDEPENDENCE LOST

In August 1939 Soviet Russia and Nazi Germany signed the infamous Molotov—Ribbentrop Pact, a nonaggression treaty that was to seal the fate of Estonia, Latvia, and Lithuania for the next 50 years: The Baltic states, along with parts of Poland and Finland, were to become Soviet territories in exchange for Soviet noninterference when Germany invaded western Poland.

Estonia was soon occupied by 100,000 Soviet troops. Thousands of Estonians, including Päts and other political leaders, were deported to far-flung parts of the Soviet Union. In August 1941 Estonia was officially incorporated into the Union of Soviet Socialist Republics (USSR) as a constituent republic, bringing an end to its short-lived independence.

WORLD WAR II

In June 1941 Nazi Germany invaded the Soviet Union. By the end of August the Germans had swept through the Baltic states and captured the whole of mainland Estonia. By the end of the year they had advanced within a short distance of Moscow. The Germans were welcomed as liberators in Estonia, until it became obvious they were an occupation force. About 1,000 Estonian Jews were murdered, and an additional 6,000 Estonians were executed. Thousands of Estonians were deported to Germany as forced labor, and a puppet administration was set up to rule the country. From 1942 the Germans began recruiting thousands of Estonians to fight against the Soviets in a special Estonian legion.

The Soviets began a series of offensives following their victory at the Battle of Stalingrad (1942—43). By July 1944 the Soviet army had recaptured much of European Russia and had reached the Estonian border at Narva. Faced with the prospect of renewed Soviet occupation, the leader of the Estonian resistance, Jüri Uluots (1890—1945), called for Estonians to defend the city. For more than six months, 45,000 Estonians fought alongside the Germans in an attempt to stop the Soviet advance. By September 1944, however, the Red Army had again conquered Estonia. Many Estonians fled west or to Sweden to avoid living under Soviet rule.

SOVIET OPPRESSION

War casualties, deportations, and fleeing refugees reduced Estonia's population from a prewar level of 1.13 million to 850,000 by the end of the 1940s. An anti-Russian resistance continued to fight from forest bases but was unsuccessful against the might of the Soviet army.

This Soviet war memorial along the coastal Pirita Tee honors the millions who suffered or died during the regime.

The 1950s were a difficult time for Estonians, and many people suffered under Soviet dictator Joseph Stalin's harsh regime: Political opponents, intellectuals, and anyone believed to be a German collaborator were deported to Siberian labor camps. The total number deported was around 60,000. The Soviet administration also introduced cultural Russification in a systematic attempt to eradicate Estonian national consciousness. Estonian history was rewritten, national monuments destroyed, and books suppressed.

Despite Soviet oppression, Estonian national consciousness remained strong. In the post-Stalin era, Estonians began to demonstrate for civil rights. Dissent in the Baltic states reached its height in 1979, on the 40th anniversary of the Molotov—Ribbentrop Pact.

INDEPENDENCE REGAINED

Soviet president Mikhail Gorbachev's policies of glasnost, or openness, and perestroika, or restructuring, led to greater political freedom in Estonia. Estonian cultural life flourished, a free press developed, political parties were formed, and religion was openly practiced again. The "awakening" began with massive environmental demonstrations protesting Moscow's plans for strip mining in northern Estonia. In 1989 the Communist government of Estonia declared its "sovereignty," a move rejected by Gorbachev. After the first-ever free Soviet elections in 1990, the new government of Estonia declared independence on March 30, 1990.

In August 1991 a failed military coup in Moscow by Communist hard-liners effectively ousted Gorbachev and led to the breakup of the Soviet Union. Estonia declared full independence on August 20, 1991. It declined to join the successor to the USSR, the Commonwealth of Independent States (CIS), preferring to sever ties with Russia.

Since independence, Estonia has embraced a multiparty parliamentary-style democracy that has relied heavily on coalitions to form governments. Despite a number of parliamentary scandals, Estonian democracy has thrived as the economy has grown from strength to strength. Estonia has become more integrated with the culture and economy of Western Europe, with the government achieving its long-term aim of joining the EU in 2004, as well as joining NATO the same year.

"The miserable house in which he lives is not his own. The field which he cultivates by the sweat of his brow, and the fruit, do not belong to him. All that he has–his flock, servant, even his wife and children, are the property of his master."
–Johann Christoph Petri, describing the life of the Estonian serf in *Ehstland und die Ehsten* (1802)

GOVERNMENT

The Estonian parliament, or Riigikogu, building in Tallinn.

CHAPTER 3

SINCE GAINING INDEPENDENCE from the Soviet Union in 1991, Estonia has had to build a new system of government, a task that the country has achieved with remarkable success in a short time. The Estonian government consists of an elected president, who is the head of state, and a single legislative assembly, the Riigikogu, led by the prime minister, who is the head of the government.

There have been frequent changes of prime minister and various realignments of government coalitions since independence. Between 1991 and 2008, there were six parliaments and 11 changes of government. Despite this apparent political instability, government policy on political and economic reform remained consistent, and reforms continued at a rapid pace. Estonian democracy has the confidence of the people and enjoys a great deal of popular support. Much of this support is a result of Estonia's highly successful transformation to a free-market economy. A new legal framework for business was quickly established, while a civil code for property plus laws on competition, enterprise, and bankruptcy were introduced.

A girl waves the national flag during an election rally in Tallinn.

In 1988 the Estonian Supreme Soviet, the country's local communist government, declared limited political sovereignty. A pro-independence party, the Estonian Popular Front (EPF), gained seats in the Estonian Supreme Soviet in 1990. A parallel ruling body, the Congress of Estonia, was formed by more-radical parties demanding a restitution of the independent republic. Edgar Savisaar became the prime minister of the Supreme Soviet. Estonia's name, flag, and anthem were restored, although the Soviet leadership declared them invalid. A national referendum was held in March 1991, and 78 percent of Estonians (including some ethnic minorities) responded in favor of independence.

Estonia and many other Soviet republics declared their independence in August 1991, as soon as the coup in Moscow failed. This led to the immediate disintegration of the USSR.

Internet voting is used in elections in Estonia. The first Internet voting took place in the 2005 local elections, and the first in a parliamentary election was in 2007, when 30,275 Estonians voted electronically. Estonia is the first country in the world to allow Internet voting in a national election.

The Estonian government is keen to avoid being tainted with accusations of corruption or unfair dealing, allegations often leveled at fledgling administrations in post-Communist Eastern Europe. Any suspected offenses are swiftly dealt with. For example, an Estonian ministry official was dismissed from his post for using his ministry cars to transport his wife and children on unofficial business.

POLITICS SINCE INDEPENDENCE

With a great many parties contesting elections since independence, coalition government has become the norm in Estonian politics. Estonia's current political system dates from 1992, when a new constitution was adopted following a referendum, which provided for a 101-seat parliament, the Riigikogu, and a presidency with limited powers. Estonia's first free parliamentary elections were held in September of the same year, with 38 parties participating. The conservative Fatherland alliance won 29 seats, making it the largest party in the Riigikogu. The leader of the Fatherland alliance, Mart Laar, became prime minister of a coalition government.

The new center-right government possessed few links with the old Soviet establishment. Several ministers were younger than 35 years old, while many others were recently returned émigrés, or refugees. Following a series of scandals and political defections, Laar was forced to resign as prime minister in 1994. He was replaced by Andres Tarand, leader of the moderates.

Estonia's second postindependence parliamentary election, held in 1995, was contested by 30 parties. Forty-one seats were won by an alliance of the Estonian Coalition Party and the Rural Union. A coalition of the newly established Estonian Reform Party won 19 seats, and the Estonian Center Party gained 16 seats. For the first time, the Russian minority was represented in the Riigikogu, by the Our Home Is Estonia alliance, which won six seats. Tilt Vähi, leader of the Estonian Coalition Party, became prime minister. Vähi resigned as prime minister on February 25, 1997, following allegations of corrupt real estate dealings in Tallinn. The deputy chairman of the Estonian Coalition Party, Mart Siimann, a former journalist, was nominated the new prime minister.

A woman casts her vote during the 2007 national elections.

In parliamentary elections in 1999, the People's Party Moderates formed a coalition with Mart Laar as prime minister. In January 2002 Laar stepped down again, and Siim Kallas was appointed prime minister, leading a coalition of the Reform Party and the Center Party. Juhan Parts led a coalition of the Res Publica Party, the Estonian Reform Party, and the People's Union to form a government following the parliamentary election in 2003. Parts resigned in 2005 following a no-confidence vote in the Riigikogu against one of his ministers, and the president nominated Estonian Reform Party leader Andrus Ansip as prime minister. Ansip formed a new government, the eighth in 12 years. The most recent parliamentary elections were held in 2007, with Prime Minister Ansip's Reform Party again winning the most votes.

THE PRESIDENT

The president of the republic is the head of state. The president is elected for a term of five years by a secret ballot in the Riigikogu and must gain a two-thirds majority. Presidential candidates must be Estonian citizens and at least 40 years old. The president's duties are mainly ceremonial, including representing Estonia in international relations and carrying out various diplomatic duties. The president is also responsible for initiating amendments to the constitution, declaring elections for the Riigikogu, and nominating candidates for the post of the prime minister.

Estonia's first presidential elections, held in fall 1992, were inconclusive; no candidate won a majority, but four main candidates emerged. Following a second round of voting, Lennart Meri was declared the winner. Meri, an intellectual famous for his films and writings on Estonian history and culture, held the position until 2001. In 2001, Arnold Rüütel was elected president, holding the position for one term. In 2006, Toomas Hendrik Ilves became Estonia's current president. An experienced politician, Ilves is a former diplomat and journalist, was the leader of the Social Democratic Party in the 1990s, and later became a member of the European Parliament. Estonia's next presidential elections will be held in 2011.

Toomas Hendrik Ilves became president of Estonia in 2006.

Presidents since independence: Lennart Meri, 1992-2001. Arnold Rüütel, 2001-06 Toomas Hendrik Ilves, 2006-present.

THE RIIGIKOGU

Legislative power rests with Estonia's state assembly, the Riigikogu. The Riigikogu's 101 members are elected for a term of four years by a system of proportional representation. They must be 21 years or older. Estonian citizens over the age of 18 can vote in national elections and referendums. The Riigikogu adopts laws, decides on the holding of referendums, elects the president of the republic, and ratifies the national budget. The Riigikogu also elects from its members a chairman who directs the work and procedures of the assembly.

Estonia's parliament (Riigikogu) in an opening session in Tallinn.

Executive power is held by the Council of Ministers, which is formed from members of the Riigikogu. The Council of Ministers consists of the prime minister, who is the head of the government, and other ministers. The prime minister has the task of forming the Council of Ministers, whose members are usually selected from the leading political parties. The Council of Ministers implements policy decisions and legislation, coordinates the work of government institutions, submits draft legislation to the Riigikogu, and organizes relations with foreign states.

POLITICAL PARTIES

Eleven parties ran in the most recent election, in 2007, and six of these gained seats in the Riigikogu; the ruling Estonian Reform Party and the Estonian Center Party (which are both liberal parties, the latter being very popular among Russian voters), the conservative Union of Pro Patria and Res Publica, the Social Democratic Party, the Estonian Greens, and the rural-based People's Union of Estonia.

At the World Congress of Finno-Ugric Peoples in 2008, Estonian president Toomas Hendrik Ilves met Russian president Dmitry Medvedev, marking the first official meeting between presidents of the two countries since the collapse of the Soviet Union.

For a party to be legally registered, it must have at least 1,000 members. In elections a party must gain at least 5 percent of the vote to be awarded a seat in the Riigikogu. Most of the larger political parties campaign on the basis of a complete economic and social program, while smaller parties, such as the ethnic Russian Party in Estonia, represent the interests of a particular group or campaign on a single issue.

LOCAL GOVERNMENT

Under Soviet administration, there were no local governing bodies. Since independence, Estonia has introduced a system of local government. Local government is divided into counties, towns, and rural municipalities. Local bodies are split into 15 *maakonnad*, or counties, plus six cities: Tallinn, Tartu, Narva, Kohtla-Järve, Pärnu, and Sillamäe. Estonia practices a single-tier system of local government, with county councils acting as representatives of the national government at a regional level.

The local government carries out administrative functions, manages state property, and provides services. The increase of local government responsibilities has been severely hampered by a lack of finances. Local government is funded by the national government. All Estonian citizens can vote in local elections, as can residents who are not citizens. However, only citizens can run for office.

JUSTICE

Justice is administered solely by Estonia's courts. Rural and city courts hear cases at the local level. District courts can review the decisions of the lower courts, and the Supreme Court, the highest court in the land, is the ultimate court of appeal. Judges are appointed by the president, and they remain judges for life.

As in most other democracies, all defendants in Estonia are assumed innocent until proven guilty, and all defendants have the right to legal representation in court. The constitution provides that all court proceedings be held in public. Suspects can be held for 48 hours without being formally charged, while further detention requires a court order. Suspects can be arrested only with a warrant issued by a court. Estonia's police force was formed in 1991 from the remnants of the Soviet militia and comes under the Ministry of Internal Affairs.

ARMED FORCES

Following the breakup of the Soviet Union, Estonia did not have an army. Russia maintained military bases in Estonia until 1994. In April 1992, Estonia established its own Ministry of Defense and an independent military, with the military firmly under civilian control. According to the constitution, the president is the supreme commander of the armed forces.

The courthouse in Tallinn.

Estonia's armed forces number around 3,800 personnel; most are in the army. Military service is for 12 months. Estonia also has an estimated 8,000 reserves, known as the Voluntary Defense League, plus a paramilitary border guard of 2,000 men and women under the command of the Ministry of the Interior. Russia's northern region forces are many times greater, but Estonia's membership in NATO ensures wider support from other military forces in Europe and beyond. Since the mid-1990s, Estonia has sent troops on peacekeeping missions, in particular to Afghanistan and Kosovo. Estonia has also supported the United States in its recent overseas military operations and contributed a force to the occupation of Iraq in 2005, although all Estonian troops were withdrawn in 2009 to be redeployed to Afghanistan. Estonia joined NATO in March 2004. Most Estonians support their country's membership in NATO, since it offers them protection against more powerful neighbors. Most recently, NATO established its Cooperative Cyber Defense Center of Excellence in Estonia.

Estonia, like the other Baltic states, has actively sought greater integration with Western Europe. It successfully negotiated membership in the EU and NATO, both of which it joined in 2004. Membership in the EU and NATO has helped the country's economy and ensured Estonia's long-term security.

Since Estonia became independent from the Soviet Union, relations with its large and powerful neighbor have been fractious. Russia recognized Estonian independence after the failed coup attempt in Moscow in August 1991, and diplomatic relations were established later that year.

One of the first points of conflict was Estonia's introduction of a citizenship law that did not automatically recognize ethnic Russians as citizens. Large numbers of Russians had moved to Estonia in the Soviet period, from 1941 to 1991. Estonia's Russians were required to undergo a naturalization process that included a basic-level Estonian language exam and test about the constitution. Social security was the same for all persons, citizens or not, and Estonia allowed noncitizens to vote in local but not national elections. These policies aimed to gradually integrate Russians into Estonia's postindependence society. Russia claimed that its people were being discriminated against, and it linked troop withdrawals to what it saw as fair treatment of the Russian minority. In January 1992 some 25,000 troops were reported left in Estonia, with more than 150 battle tanks, 300 armored vehicles, and 163 military aircrafts. The deadlock continued until August 1994, when the last Soviet troops finally departed Estonia, but the dispute left a bitter diplomatic legacy.

Estonia and Russia also have a long-running border dispute relating to 772 square miles (2,000 square km) of land annexed by Stalin's government in 1945. Negotiators reached an agreement on the border in 1996, and in May 2005, after a decade of talks, Estonia and Russia signed a treaty defining the border between the two countries. The Estonian parliament ratified it soon afterward, but only after it had introduced a reference to the former Soviet occupation. The Russians were unhappy about this addition and pulled out of the treaty, saying that talks would have to begin afresh.

More recently, in 2007, the two countries were at loggerheads over the relocation of the Bronze Soldier of Tallinn and the bodies buried beneath the monument. Erected in 1947, the monument is a memorial to the Soviet soldiers who helped liberate Tallinn from Nazi occupation during World War II. The Estonian government moved the monument and bodies to a less conspicuous site in the Defense Forces Cemetery of Tallinn. The Russian government saw this act as disrespecting the heroism and honor of the Red Army's war dead. The controversy caused Russians to demonstrate outside the Estonian embassy in Moscow for a week and led to riots in Tallinn. Russia subsequently suspended transportation of oil through Estonian ports, which many believed was retaliation for the removal of the war memorial. For several days that year, the websites of Estonian organizations, including the parliament, banks, ministries, newspapers, and broadcasters, were swamped and virtually disabled by a series of massive cyber attacks. Some observers were of the opinion that the attacks originated from Russian hackers. The attacks had important implications for Estonia's defense network and banking systems.

Estonia's relations with its Baltic and Scandinavian neighbors have been far more positive and productive. Since independence, Estonia has sought to re-create its traditional and historical ties with the Nordic countries, especially Finland and Sweden. The Baltic Assembly (BA) was established in 1991 as a forum for the governments of Estonia, Latvia, and Lithuania to discuss common economic, political, and cultural issues. The BA is made up of 60 members—20 from each country. In 1994 another body, the Baltic Council of Ministers, was set up to allow for direct minister-to-minister contact between the governments of the Baltic countries.

Estonia's trade and cultural ties with Sweden, Finland, and Germany have grown during the past 15 years, and in 2005, Estonia joined the European Union's Nordic Battlegroup. The Estonian government has also shown continued interest in joining the Nordic Council. In 1992 more than 90 percent of Estonia's international trade was with Russia, whereas today three-quarters of foreign investment in Estonia comes from Finland and Sweden, to which Estonia sends more than 31 percent of its exports.

ECONOMY

The tower of SEB Eesti Uhispank in Tallinn is one of Estonia's modern architectural landmarks and an important financial hub.

CHAPTER 4

ESTONIA IS CONSIDERED ONE OF THE pioneers of the global economy in Eastern Europe and has had great success in integrating into the world economy after many decades under Communist rule.

Estonia is already rated a high-income country by the World Bank, with a gross domestic product (GDP) per capita that is fast catching up with the EU average. By most international standards, Estonia is considered an easy place to do business, with high transparency and freedom in the labor market.

Estonia had one of the fastest-growing economies in the world until 2006, with growth rates in 1997, 2000, 2005, and 2006 of more than 10 percent. Even as the global economy began to slow, Estonia's GDP still grew by 7 percent in 2007. Amid the global recession of 2008—09, Estonia's economy slowed dramatically, but the crisis was less dramatic than in other countries thanks to financial reserves saved up during the years of growth. The economy is expected to improve in 2010. Estonia's main trading partners include Sweden, Finland, and Germany, and the country's economy is heavily influenced by developments in those countries.

Joining the EU was one of the Estonian government's main foreign-policy targets after independence, and negotiations with the EU began in 1998. Many Estonians felt lukewarm about becoming a part of the EU, so leading politicians campaigned hard to persuade Estonian voters that it would be beneficial for the country. On September 14, 2003, Estonians voted on a referendum on whether to join the EU, and 66.83 percent voted in favor. Estonia became a part of the EU on May 1, 2004.

The Skype technology that allows so many people to speak to each other for free using a microphone and their telephone line was developed in Estonia in 2003. The business was later acquired by eBay, which markets the software worldwide.

FROM COMMUNISM TO CAPITALISM

Historically Estonia had an agricultural economy. Industrial development in the 1930s changed this, as did the forced collectivization of farms and further industrialization under the Soviets in the 1940s and 1950s. All property and industry were nationalized under Soviet rule. For 50 years Estonia's economy was centrally controlled and directed from Moscow as an integral part of the Soviet Union. Decisions concerning the country's economic and industrial development were made within the context of the whole USSR, and Estonia was subservient to Moscow's broader plans for the USSR as a whole.

Estonia's transformation from a centrally controlled, Soviet-style economy to a free-market economy has been miraculously fast. Estonia began the transition to a market economy in the late 1980s with the establishment of a central bank and a private banking system. By mid-1994, only three years after independence, the private sector was generating more than 50 percent of Estonia's GDP. This transformation has not occurred without some suffering for the Estonian people. The winter of 1991—92 was probably the hardest Estonians have experienced since World War II, with the cost of living increasing tenfold by the end of 1992. This was particularly hard for the people to bear, as Estonia had been one of the wealthiest regions in the USSR before independence.

Shoppers in the Tallinna Kaubamaja mall in Tallinn.

In 1994, Estonia became one of the first countries in the world to adopt a flat tax rate, where all workers, regardless of income, pay the same percentage of tax.

TRADE

Estonia has a well-educated, technically skilled workforce and lower wage rates compared with many of its competitors in Western Europe, making the country very attractive to foreign investors. Companies from Europe and the United States have invested extensively in its timber, textile, and manufacturing industries. Estonia's neighbors Sweden and Finland have been two of its biggest investors and have purchased many of Estonia's newly privatized companies. Major American and Finnish corporations have also invested in the computer, electronics, and automobile industries.

An aerial view of Muuga Port in Tallinn.

During the past 15 years, the Estonian economy has enjoyed an export-led boom, especially in machinery and equipment, wood and paper, textiles, furniture, metals, and chemical products. Estonia exports goods chiefly to Finland (18 percent), Sweden (13 percent), Latvia (11.4 percent), Russia (9 percent), and Germany (5.2 percent).

Estonia's main sources of imported goods are Finland (15.9 percent), Germany (12.8 percent), Russia (10 percent), and Sweden (10 percent). At one time 70 percent of Estonia's trade was with the Russian Federation, but this has fallen dramatically, in large part because of Estonia's membership in the EU.

FINANCE

In recent years Tallinn has emerged as a financial center, with a number of local and international banks having offices there. Estonia was the first former Soviet republic to introduce its own currency, the kroon (meaning "crown"), in June 1992. The kroon is divided into 100 senti (singular: sent). The kroon has proved to be a remarkably strong and stable currency and has delivered Estonia from the raging inflation that existed when it was using the Russian ruble. The kroon is also a part of the EU's exchange rate mechanism, which means it has a fixed conversion against the main EU currency, the euro.

The average annual income in Estonia in 2007 was $21,800.

Of the total labor force, almost 60 percent work in service categories and 38 percent in industry. The number of people employed in agriculture has decreased dramatically.

AGRICULTURE AND INDUSTRY

Approximately 70,000 Estonians, or 2 percent of the labor force, are employed in the agricultural sector. Combined with fishing, agriculture contributes only approximately 3 percent of the country's industrial output, down from 10 percent in 1997 and in marked contrast to Estonia's traditional role Oas an agrarian economy. For centuries Estonians referred to themselves as *maarahvas* (MAH- rahh-vus), meaning "people of the land," and the farming lifestyle became a part of the Estonian identity. In the 1930s, the heyday of Estonian agriculture, it was popularly thought that Estonian eggs, butter, and meat graced the breakfast tables of Saint Petersburg and London.

In the Soviet era, Estonia's farms were forcibly collectivized and brought under government control. All traditional family farms were nationalized, and many farmers and their families were deported to Siberia. By 1949, Estonia's 140,000 farms had been converted into 2,400 state-run units. In the 1990s the process was reversed, with farms being privatized, reorganized, and reinstated to their former family-run status. Inefficiency remains a problem for Estonia's farms, and farmers have difficulty financing the purchase of modern farming equipment. Consequently, overall agricultural production steadily declined through the 1990s, and many farmers struggle to do more than break even.

A sheep farm in Ullaste in western Estonia.

A farmer uses modern machinery to harvest his crops on a farm in central Estonia.

Barley, other grains, potatoes, and other vegetables are the principal crops grown. Dairy farms are numerous, and meat, milk, eggs, and butter are the country's chief agricultural products. Estonia's food processing industry meets domestic demand and accounts for 9 percent of exports.

FORESTRY Estonia's forests, which cover 40 percent of the country, are an obvious natural resource. The exploitation of these forests provides timber for furniture manufacturing, pulp factories, paper goods, and fuel.

Estonians' timber skills and low wage levels have made the country's timber industry highly competitive and successful, with wood and paper products making up 15 percent of exports.

ENGINEERING AND ELECTRONICS Estonia's engineering and electronics industry has grown rapidly since independence, fueled by extensive foreign investment. In 2007, 15,000 skilled technicians were employed in the electronics sector by approximately 370 companies. Over the past 10 years, output has grown fifteenfold, with the electronics industry taking in 238 million euros in 2001, rising to 719 million euros by 2006. In 2006

Most urban Estonians make a trip to the country every summer. Southern Estonia and the islands are the most popular rural destinations, while Pärnu is the most visited city.

The Mollatsi Bog in Tartumaa, where peat mining began in 2002.

the electronics industry contributed 11 percent of total industrial output. Products include electronic motors, integrated circuits, cables, and other high-tech products. Factories formerly working for the Soviet military have been successfully adapted to sell to Western markets.

TEXTILES Estonia's thriving textile industry has adjusted quickly to the demands of a market economy. Estonia exports clothing and footwear products to the rest of Europe and the United States. The textile industry contributes 14 percent of total exports.

CHEMICALS AND MINING The mining industry makes up 1 percent of Estonia's GDP. Mined resources include oil shale, peat, and industrial minerals such as clays, limestone, sand, and gravel. Estonia has large phosphorite deposits, which are the basis of the fertilizer manufacturing industry. The chemical industry, which contributes more than 10 percent of Estonia's industrial output, produces household chemical products, fertilizers, plastics, paints, and lacquer products.

ENERGY

In the past Estonia was heavily dependent on Soviet energy supplies. Since independence, the oil-shale industry, centered around Kohtla-Järve, Kiviõli, and Narva, has become Estonia's main source of domestic and industrial energy, making the country virtually independent in electricity production and providing 14 percent of its industrial output. Estonia has abundant supplies of oil shale, estimated at 16.5 billion tons (15 billion metric tons). Most of the oil shale is used to supply thermal power plants, which in turn generate electricity, some of which is then exported to Latvia, the Netherlands, Finland, and Denmark. Estonia also imports small amounts of natural gas from Russia.

Peat and firewood are significant energy sources as well, as are two hydroelectric plants on the Narva River. The government is actively seeking ways to upgrade the thermal power plants to control pollution and limit damage to the environment.

SERVICES AND TOURISM

Estonia's service industry is the best developed in the former Soviet Union and is one of the country's biggest growth industries. It has developed rapidly since independence and today accounts for almost 65 percent of total GDP. The service sector employs nearly 60 percent of the Estonian workforce,

According to an Estonian survey, in 2007 half of all Estonians made at least one trip abroad lasting more than a day. Finland is the most popular country to visit, while other popular destinations include Egypt, Spain, Turkey, Greece, and Italy.

Crude-oil terminals in Talinn.

The Saltsjon and Viking Line passenger cruise ships at the Masthamnen docks.

especially in telecommunications, information technology (IT), and financial services. Tourism has been growing since 1990, particularly during the past 15 years. Foreigners and local residents visit the historic towns of Tallinn and Tartu and experience the tranquility of the rural interior and the coastal resorts and islands of Hiiumaa and Saaremaa.

It is estimated that 2.5 million foreigners visited Estonia in 2008, and domestic tourists accounted for more than a million visits, with tourism producing nearly 15 percent of Estonia's GDP. The vast majority of international visitors were from neighboring Finland, though significant numbers came from Latvia, Russia, Germany, and Sweden. Ferries have been crossing the Gulf of Finland since 1936, and many Finns take day trips from Helsinki to Tallinn to shop for cheaper goods and see the sights of the Estonian capital. Since independence, there has been a rapid increase in hotels, bed-and-breakfasts, and home stays organized by Western travel agents.

TRANSPORTATION

Approximately 8 percent of the country's workforce is employed in transportation, which accounts for more than 10 percent of Estonia's annual GDP. Estonia gets a lot of business from traffic between Western Europe and Russia. Estonia has good road and rail links with Russia and other parts of the CIS. This makes trade and communication with other former Soviet

> THE ESTONIAN FERRY DISASTER

On September 28, 1994, the Estonian passenger ferry Estonia *capsized off the coast of Finland, killing 859 people. It was Europe's worst postwar shipping disaster. The ferry was en route from Tallinn to Stockholm with 1,040 passengers and crew when it encountered strong gales and waves 33 feet (10 m) high. Water flooded the car deck. The weight of the water and the unchained vehicles caused the ferry to list heavily to one side and eventually sink at 2 A.M.*

The official report suggests that weak locks and the faulty design of the bow doors caused them to be forced open in bad weather and rolling seas, letting water into the car deck. However, the German builders of the ferry reject the official findings. Conspiracy theories are rife, suggesting that Estonia *was carrying a smuggled cargo of narcotics or a consignment of high-tech military equipment. Poor seamanship or bad design are the most likely causes, but as yet, no definitive explanation has been discovered.*

countries easy and allows Estonia to act as a bridge between the other Baltic countries and Russia, as well as beyond into the Central Asian republics. The Via Baltika is a 416-mile (670-km) highway that connects Tallinn with the Polish capital of Warsaw and the Czech Republic capital of Prague, offering a continuous road from the Baltic coast into Central Europe. It is the most important road connection of the Baltic states. The highway is mostly single lane, but there are plans to upgrade it to a multilane road.

If traveling by public transportation, most Estonians choose to go by bus, with daily buses from Tallinn to virtually every town and village in the country. In recent years Estonia's passenger rail network has been cut back, with few regular services beyond the suburbs of Tallinn and less frequent long-distance services to Tartu, Pärnu, and Rakvere. There are daily international services to Saint Petersburg and Moscow.

Estonia's main ports—Tallinn, Pärnu, Kunda, and Sillamäe—are vital to the country's transportation system, providing a historic gateway from Western Europe that leads deep into Russia and beyond. A number of ferries, hydrofoils, and catamarans cross the Gulf of Finland to Helsinki each day, and there is a daily ferry service to the Swedish capital of Stockholm.

International airlines such as Air Baltic, SAS, Finnair, Lufthansa, EasyJet, and Estonian Air provide direct flights to 27 destinations from Tallinn.

ENVIRONMENT

Water lilies float serenely in a bog pool in Estonia as evening light streams in.

THROUGHOUT THE BALTIC STATES, environmental pollution became a serious problem in the 1970s, and this continued into the postindependence 1990s. Much of this damage was the result of poorly planned urban and industrial expansion under the Soviet regime.

In the Communist era there was very little concern for the natural environment, and pollution went unchecked in every corner of the Soviet Union. To some extent Estonia is still dealing with the consequences of this environmental neglect. More recently, Estonia's postindependence economic boom, especially the development of the oil-shale mining and timber industries, has also had a damaging impact on the environment.

The Soviet regime did have some positive environmental side effects, however. Inefficient farming methods caused an increase in woodland, providing habitats for local wildlife. In addition, many coastal areas were out-of-bounds for military reasons, and so many beautiful beaches and coastal reedbeds remained unspoiled for 50 years. The wetlands of Estonia's coasts and islands, as well as the peat bogs and forests of the mainland, were able to develop as sustainable environments for local wildlife.

A close-up of the small plants found in the bogs of Estonia.

In 2008, after 10 years of cleanup work on a radioactive-waste site in Sillamäe, cooperation among Estonia, the Scandinavian countries, and the EU removed one of the greatest threats of pollution to the Baltic Sea. The project was started in response to the huge environmental hazard the old Soviet-era waste posed and has been a model of international cooperation.

Today the purest air and water are found in the western islands and the most polluted in the northeast, near the towns of Narva and Kohtla-Järve. In the northeast of the country, Estonia's oil-shale-burning power plants cause much air pollution by sending excessive levels of sulphur dioxide into the atmosphere. The waterways, coasts, and lakes of northern Estonia have also been polluted by waste material from oil-shale mining. This situation has dramatically improved in recent years, though; the amount of wastewater discharged today is only one-twentieth of the levels in the 1980s.

INDUSTRIAL POLLUTION

Much of the pollution has been caused by Estonia's attempt to become self-sufficient for its energy. The county of Ida-Virumaa, in the northeast of Estonia, is heavily polluted as a consequence of the oil-shale mining and power plants that are crucial to meeting Estonia's energy needs. Oil shale is used to provide power to Estonian homes and industry and has allowed the country to become almost entirely self-sufficient in power generation since independence. Oil shale is extracted through surface mining, which in itself is a dirty process that damages the land and the local environment. The crushing and loading of oil shale causes noise pollution and spreads dust, while the processing of oil shale uses up huge amounts of water.

An aerial view of an Estonian oil-shale mine.

More than 19.8 million tons (18 million metric tons) of oil shale are burned in thermal power plants at Narva each year, emitting 379,923 tons (344,660 metric tons) of sulphur dioxide. This gas not only pollutes the air in northeastern Estonia but is also carried across by the wind to the Gulf of Finland, where it pollutes Finland's forests.

After oil shale has been mined, mining waste such as spent shale and ash has to be disposed of. The waste material usually takes up a larger area than the material extracted and so cannot easily be buried underground. It is calculated that in Estonia the mining of 1 billion tons (907 million metric tons) of oil shale creates approximately 360—370 million tons (327—336 million metric tons) of solid waste, of which 90 million tons (82 million metric tons) are mining waste, 70—80 million tons (64—73 million metric tons) are semicoke, and 200 million tons (181 million metric tons) are ash.

To avoid contaminating groundwater, toxic solid waste—such as heavy metals and sulfates—are disposed of in landfills. The oil-shale mines around Kohtla-Järve have created great slag heaps, and the landscape is dotted with hills made from the ash from the oil-shale power plants. Rain washes the toxic metals and organic compounds of these mountains of waste into the sea. As a result, the waters of this part of Estonia are so polluted, no swimming or fishing is allowed in the local lakes and rivers.

Estonia is committed to developing cleaner technology to save the ecology of the northeast region, although this is proving to be an expensive project.

Radioactive waste from uranium mining in Estonia.

WATER POLLUTION

The shallow Baltic Sea is currently so polluted that Estonian fishing vessels are forced to travel to all parts of the globe to stay in business. Overfishing during the Soviet period also depleted the fish stocks drastically. The Baltic Sea has been the dumping ground for industrial waste for decades. For example, water quality in Riga, the capital of neighboring Latvia, was so bad that in 1989 there was an outbreak of hepatitis A; for many years afterward, Latvians boiled water for consumption.

In 2004 the United Nation's International Maritime Organization named the Baltic Sea as a Particularly Sensitive Sea Area (PSSA)—one of only 12 PSSAs in the world—because of its high level of pollution. As a new member of the EU, Estonia has been committed to cleaning up its waterways and upgrading its sewage system.

AIR POLLUTION

Oil-shale-fired power plants also cause air pollution, sending nitrogen oxides, sulfur dioxide, and hydrogen chloride as well as ash into the air. The mining

A sign warning people of the polluted water in a once-thriving beach along the Baltic Sea. Waste from nearby industries has polluted the area, so the seawater does not meet standards, and swimming is not advised.

of oil shale gives off more carbon dioxide emissions than does conventional oil production.

A view of the beautiful woodlands in the Haanja Landscape Reserve in Estonia.

Estonia signed the 1997 Kyoto Protocol, which targets the reduction of greenhouse gases. The Estonian government has introduced legislation that punishes companies that do not handle industrial waste properly. The government has worked hard to reduce pollution, and in 2000, emissions were 80 percent less than in 1980.

NATIONAL PARKS AND PROTECTED AREAS

Because its population is small and thinly spread, Estonia has many wetlands, forests, bogs, and coasts undisturbed by human activity. The Estonian government has made a firm attempt to protect the country's natural heritage. There are five national parks and many other protected nature reserves. The five national parks are Matsalu (120,118 acres/48,610 ha), Vilsandi (92 square miles/238 square km), Soomaa (91,847 acres/37,169 ha), Lahemaa (280 square miles/725 square km), and Karula (47 square miles/ 123 square km).

NATURE RESERVES

Although there are a number of nature reserves in Estonia, Lahemaa is the country's primary national park. Established in 1971 as the first national park in the Soviet Union, it covers an area of 280 square miles (725 square km) on the northern coast. Characterized by four evenly spaced peninsulas protruding into the Gulf of Finland, the park includes offshore islands and waters, coastal peninsulas and bays, beaches, forests, and peat bogs, as well as 14 lakes, eight rivers, and numerous waterfalls. It is home to elk, brown bears, lynx, cranes, mink, and migrating black storks. The park also contains a wealth of the huge boulders that dot the landscape of northern Estonia. These stones, carried here by glaciers 10,000 years ago, were recognized as natural monuments in the 1800s. The tallest of these is Tammispea, which is massive and 26 feet (8 m) high.

The Matsalu on Estonia's western coast, south of Haapsalu, is a superb bird habitat, with reedbeds, water meadows, and coastal pastures. Species such as the avocet, the Sandwich tern, the mute swan, and the greylag goose can be found here. The reserve was established in 1957.

There are also nature reserves in the Otepää and Haanja highlands. The Haanja Plateau is covered with wetlands and bogs and is home to many migratory birds, such as storks. The Otepää Highlands have a varied landscape that includes lakes, rivers, and forests.

One of the numerous protected marsh wetlands in Estonia.

The patchwork of grasslands, peat bogs, and forests of the Soomaa National Park is home to elk, beavers, brown bears, and flying squirrels. Formed around four coastal peninsulas in the north of the country, Lahemaa is Estonia's largest nature reserve. About 70 percent of the territory is made up of forest; not surprisingly, the park is home to a rich variety of woodland life, including roe deer, wild boars, moose, hares, martens, lynx, badgers, and beavers.

PROTECTED WETLANDS

Estonia has 12 areas of protected wetlands, which are important breeding grounds for fish and birds as well as ideal stop-off points for migrating waterfowl. North of Tartu, the Alam-Pedja Nature Reserve (64 acres/26 ha) is a flat wilderness of bogs, floodplains, and rivers that support a multitude of wildlife. Also in Tartumaa is the Emajõgi Suursoo Mire Reserve, where the swamps and reedbeds are important spawning grounds for various amphibian and fish species. The area is also vital for the hydrology (circulation and runoff water) of nearby Lake Peipsi. The much larger Soomaa National Park is a great floodplain with some of the best bogs and marshes in Estonia. In the northeast, the Muraka Nature Reserve is one of the few wilderness areas to remain in this highly industrialized area; it is home to the peregrine falcon and other birds of prey.

The mute swan is one of the numerous coastal birds that have made its home in the wetlands of Estonia.

On Estonia's west coast, Matsalu Bay is one of the biggest stop-over points for migrating birds in northern Europe. A part of the national park, the Matsalu Nature Reserve was established in 1957. It is made up of coastal reedbeds, water meadows, and islets. It is a very important site for nesting waterbirds, such as the common crane, the whooper swan, the greylag goose, and numerous breeds of duck. The area is also home to more than 700 plant species (six of which are protected). Other nature reserves on the west coast include the Sookuninga Nature Reserve and the Puhto-Laelatu-Nehatu Wetland Complex. The Sookuninga reserve supports the highly endangered and protected black stork, golden eagle, great-spotted eagle, and willow grouse. Both reserves play a very important role in maintaining groundwater quality in southwestern Estonia and northern Latvia.

The islets of Hiiumaa Island are home to rare species of orchids as well as endangered broad-leafed forests, and they support important numbers of migrating birds. The Vilsandi National Park is formed around the small island of Vilsandi off the west coast of Saaremaa Island and covers a large area of coastal reedbeds, forests, and farmland in the northwest of Saaremaa Island as well. Nearly one third of the plant species here are rare for Estonia, and many are endangered. More than 200 species of birds use the park for breeding and wintering. Also on the island of Saaremaa, the tiny Laidevahe Nature Reserve is a refuge for many threatened and endangered plant and bird species, including the barnacle goose, and is recognized by the International Union for the Conservation of Nature (IUCN) as a biosphere of international importance.

ENDANGERED ANIMALS

MAMMALS Of the 64 species of mammals identified in Estonia, the IUCN has listed 17 as threatened. The European mink is considered the most endangered animal, with few sightings in recent years, while the flying squirrel, which is common throughout the forests of Russia, and the marbled seal are classified as vulnerable. Many rare breeds of bats are also considered vulnerable. Three mammals have been introduced into the environment by humans—the muskrat, the raccoon dog, and the American mink. Another two mammals—the European beaver and the red deer—have been reintroduced after becoming threatened. The main threats to Estonia's animals are road traffic, hunting, timber and forestry work, the drainage of some wetlands, and peat bog harvesting.

BIRDS A quarter of the birds that breed in Estonia are considered threatened, with seven endangered, eight vulnerable, and 19 rare. A substantial number of the threatened birds live in the forest, where foresting activities, such as timber harvesting, damage their habitats. Estonia is home to large numbers of black storks, which are rare in much of the rest of the world. Estonia's many peat bogs and forests are perfect breeding grounds for cranes and waders. In recent years, however, the numbers of black grouse and capercaillie have steadily declined, and the willow grouse has reached the verge of extinction. Estonia is also home to a few magnificent birds of prey, including the white-tailed eagle, the osprey, and the golden eagle, all of which have disappeared from neighboring Latvia and southern Finland.

The Piusa Sand Caves form a single, connected chamber of caves near Obinitsa, in the south of the country. The caves were excavated between 1922 and 1970, to extract sand for use in glassmaking. In 1999 the area was designated a protected nature reserve, and the caves are an important habitat for bats.

The European mink is one of the many endangered species of mammals found in Estonia.

As a country of woodlands, Estonia has always seen its forests as an important source of income, and timber is harvested in every part of the land. Between 1996 and 2001, timber harvests increased 173 percent, with forest products (raw timber, wooden furniture, paper, and building materials) accounting for 19 percent of Estonia's exports in 2001. Most timber exports go to Sweden, Finland, Germany, and the United Kingdom. Some environmentalists estimate that up to 40 percent of Estonia's timber exports are illegal and exceed the government's targets, meaning the Estonian forest is being cut down at an unsustainable rate.

In a bid to tackle this issue, the Estonian State Forest Management Center (Riigimetsa Majandamise Keskus, or RMK) has sought to strictly manage the rate of timber felling in an attempt to balance the country's environmental and economic needs. The state owns 2.6 million acres (1,063,000 ha) of land, of which 291,584 acres (118,000 ha) are strictly protected forest, and an additional 350,890 acres (142,000 ha) are specially managed to ensure that the local wildlife, environment, and material culture (such as historic buildings) are not damaged.

MARINE AND AMPHIBIOUS LIFE More than 60 species of fish live in Estonia's waters. Of freshwater fish, the sheatfish and the asp have reached the verge of extinction. The natural population of local salmon has also reached a critical size. Of amphibians, the common (brown) frog, the common toad, and the spotted newt thrive. Rare and strictly protected species include the natterjack, which lives in the coastal areas of western Estonia; the green natterjack, found in southeastern Estonia and on Piirissaar Island; and the crested newt. The amphibians' habitats have been affected by the draining of lakes, bogs, and marshes.

ENDANGERED FLORA

The IUCN estimates that roughly 20 percent of Estonia's 1,600 native plant species are threatened in some way. Twenty-seven have already become extinct; another 31 are endangered, 29 vulnerable, and 100 rare. A quarter of these threatened species grow in meadows, and many others in forests and the coastal environment. Farming activities and forestry do the most harm to Estonia's plant diversity.

Since independence, however, Estonia has been gaining an average of 19,768 acres (8,000 ha) of forest per year, at a rate of 0.37 percent annually. Between 1990 and 2005, Estonia increased its forests by 5.6 percent, or around 298,998 acres (121,000 ha). This is mostly because of tree replanting by the timber industry and environmental volunteer organizations.

A natterjack toad.

ESTONIANS

Women running along the Katariina Passage in Tallinn.

ESTONIA IS A MULTICULTURAL country of slightly more than 1.3 million people. Ethnic Estonians make up 68.6 percent of the population, while ethnic Russians are the second-largest group at 24.9 percent. The other major ethnic groups in Estonia are much smaller: Ukrainians (2.1 percent), Belarusians (1.2 percent), and Finns (0.8 percent). Other minorities include Tatars, Jews, Latvians, Poles, Lithuanians, and Germans. Estonia's minorities tend to be concentrated in the larger cities and towns.

The ethnic mixture of people in Estonia has changed drastically over the past 60 years, partly because of the loss of roughly a quarter of the population during World War II but also as a result of the Baltic country's incorporation into the Soviet Union and consequent Soviet migration policies. In the Soviet era, Estonia became home to more than 100 ethnic groups, mainly from other parts of the Soviet Union. In 1934 a census showed that 88 percent of the people in Estonia were ethnic Estonians. Recent statistics show that figures had fallen by a quarter, while the number of Russians dramatically increased from a pre-1940 figure of 8 percent to a quarter of the population today. Between

A boy plays with a toy sailboat in Tallinn.

People sitting at a sidewalk café in Tallinn's Town Hall Square.

1945 and 1990, approximately 1.4 million people, mostly Russian speaking, passed through Estonia, sometimes settling down there. Such a dense flow of people has had a corrosive effect on traditional Estonian society and has led to domestic tensions. Today it is estimated that a fifth of the country's residents were born outside of the country.

A great number of people left Estonia during the first years of independence: Polls carried out in 1989 and 2000 show that the population of Estonia decreased by at least 194,000 people, or about 12 percent, during those years. According to a 1989 census, the population was 1,565,000; by 1997 the number had fallen to 1,464,000; in 2009 the population was estimated to be even lower, at 1,299,371.

This decrease is partly due to the halt in migration from the former Soviet Union, increased migration to Western European countries after Estonia joined the EU in 2004, and a drop in the birthrate. Although many young people left to work and study in Western Europe, this trend recently reversed when the world economy slowed down, resulting in fewer opportunities in the West.

President Ilves has talked about "Yule-land," countries that share a name for Christmas. The name *Jõulud* came to Estonia from Scandinavia.

ESTONIANS

Estonians are a Finno-Ugric people, one among an ethnolinguistic group that includes the Finns, the Lapps, and the Hungarians. They first arrived in Estonia 6,000 years ago, having journeyed across the Asian landmass from the marshes of Siberia.

Estonians are not related to their Baltic neighbors, the Latvians and the Lithuanians, who are Indo-European peoples. Ethnically and culturally, Estonians are close cousins to Finns and have more in common with them than with the other Baltic people. Estonians feel themselves to be very Scandinavian and not at all linked to Slavic people.

Estonians are traditionally a rural people. In Estonia today the rural areas are dominated by ethnic Estonians, some of whom still pursue the traditional vocations of farming, forestry, and fishing. Ethnic Estonians are not evenly spread across the country: In 13 of Estonia's 15 counties, 80 percent of the people are of Estonian background, and in Hiiumaa, Estonians make up 98 percent of the population. However, in the more urban Harjumaa, which includes the capital, Tallinn, ethnic Estonians make up just 60 percent of the population, while in Ida-Virumaa in the northeast they are a minority. Among the cities, Tartu is rare in being predominantly Estonian in ethnic makeup and character.

A happy trio of children in Estonia.

CHARACTERISTICS

Estonians are typical north Europeans in that they are individualistic and enjoy solitude. This explains the popularity of country homes: In summer most Estonians like to retreat to their country houses for as long as possible. The Baltic peoples are generally calm in character and not given to great displays of passion or affection. Some visitors find Estonians cool and reserved and say they have mastered the art of being polite without being friendly. The Slavic peoples, especially the Russians, tend to be more expansive and openly affectionate, offering hugs to each other when meeting. Estonians shy away from open displays of affection and tend to negatively associate such behavior with their least favorite neighbor. For Estonians, friendship is highly prized and not easily proffered.

The town of Haapsalu is home to the Museum of Estonian Swedes, which displays traditional costumes and household textiles, as well as a tapestry telling the story of Estonia's Swedish community.

Young Estonian adults enjoying themselves on a wooden raft.

THE ESTONIAN IDENTITY

Estonians began to develop a national identity only 120 years ago, following the national revival of the late 19th century. For Estonians, ethnic identity is the essence of their nationhood. Domination by foreign powers is most apparent in the architecture of the country, which is mainly German, Swedish, and Russian in character. Many Estonian institutions were also introduced by these conquerors. Consequently Estonians have retained a sense of themselves through their traditions, language, and lifestyle. As a part of the Soviet Union, Estonians were not allowed to express their cultural separateness, except through officially recognized "Socialist realism" art forms, and were instead encouraged to adhere to the Communist Party ideal of the Soviet citizen—a "universal" human dedicated to international socialism. This ideology never appealed to the individualistic Estonians.

As a result of nationalistic feeling, Estonians have turned resolutely toward the West to find a new lifestyle and sense of purpose, one not dominated by Russia and communist ideology.

Estonians love their national symbols, probably because of the country's long history of foreign occupation. Featured on the notes and coins of the Estonian currency are Tallinn's Toompea Castle, Tartu University, Tallinn's Pikk Hermann, a mighty oak tree, and a barn swallow.

DRESS

As a result of their newfound affluence, Estonians dress very similarly to people elsewhere in the West. Long gone are the days of drab, Soviet-style suits. Western-made designer clothes can be bought in many shops in Tallinn. The long winters and cold weather mean that warm clothing is the norm; this includes heavy coats, sweaters, scarves, heavy boots, and thick socks.

Female folk dancers dressed in traditional Estonian outfits.

In Narva 93.85 percent of the population are Russian speakers, mostly Soviet-era immigrants or their descendants.

Though there are regional variations, Estonians do have a recognizable national dress. Today it is often worn on festive occasions, especially for summer song festivals. Since independence, wearing traditional dress has become increasingly popular at national celebrations as a way of visibly expressing Estonian culture. Women wear long, heavy, woven skirts, gathered at the waist. The skirts are usually red, black, yellow, or orange and decorated with either fine vertical stripes or wide horizontal bands. If a skirt with vertical stripes is worn, it is usually combined with a heavy apron. A black or patterned belt holds the apron and skirt in place.

White, long-sleeved blouses are usually worn above the skirts, with wide, lace-edged collars and cuffs. The blouses are sometimes embroidered with floral designs and motifs. The collar is often fastened with a large, ornamental pin. Sleeveless bodices are also worn. The outfit is usually worn with white stockings and black shoes. Women often wear close-fitting caps or kerchiefs made of white linen and decorated with lace and silk ribbons.

Estonian men wear black breeches, fastened at the knees with silver buttons, with a patterned vest over a white, long-sleeved shirt. The shirt is fastened at the neck with a braided tie or a pin. Sometimes a skullcap is worn on the head. Like the women, the men also wear white stockings and black shoes.

RUSSIANS

Russians make up roughly a quarter of the total population. They account for 36 percent of the population in the more urbanized Harjumaa and 70 percent of the population in Ida-Virumaa, centered around the industrial cities of Narva and Kohtla-Järve. The closing down of Russia's military bases on Estonian soil in 1994 caused many Russians to move back to Russia, with the ethnic Russian population dropping from 29 percent in 1994 to 24.9 percent today. A similar situation exists in neighboring Latvia, where Russians today make up one-third of the population.

Children of Russian descent in their school uniforms.

Some Russians have lived in the Baltic countries since the 18th century, after Russia annexed the region from Sweden in the Great Northern War. In Estonia most of these early migrants lived in villages around Lake Peipsi. Many of them were Old Believers, followers of a conservative form of Russian Orthodoxy who were persecuted in Russia proper. The vast majority of today's Russians in Estonia, however, moved to the country during the Soviet occupation. Some were encouraged to move as administrators in the Soviet government, while others moved to work in the industries of Estonia's northeast. Only about 40 percent of Estonia's Russian population were born in Estonia. Many retired Russian military personnel, especially officers, have chosen to remain in Estonia.

Today Russians have a highly visible presence in the industrial towns of northern Estonia. In Narva, the vast majority of the people are ethnic Russians, and the populations of Kohtla-Järve and Sillamäe are primarily Russian as well. As a result, Ida-Virumaa has taken on a very Russian character. Even in the capital, Tallinn, half of the population is Russian. Sociological surveys reveal that most Russians identify themselves primarily with either Russia or their local city but not with the Estonian state.

The presence of a significant Russian minority has caused problems in Estonia in the years since independence. Russians without Estonian citizenship claim they are discriminated against in the workplace or treated as second-class citizens regarding salaries and public housing. Many perceived injustices are reported frequently in the Russian mass media, which are the main source

In 2005 the Ingrian Finnish minority in Estonia elected a cultural council and was granted cultural autonomy by the government. The Estonian Swedish minority also received cultural autonomy in 2007.

of news for the Russian-speaking population, and are a source of tension between Estonia and Russia. One such incident was the relocation of a World War II memorial, the Bronze Soldier of Tallinn, in 2007.

Unfortunately a linguistic barrier still exists and hinders full integration. For 50 years Russian was the common language of the whole Soviet Union, and the Russians in Estonia did not need to learn to speak Estonian. Since independence, a knowledge of Estonian is essential for education, business, and citizenship. However, with the growth of Russian nationalism in Russia, many ethnic Russians in Estonia have been reluctant to integrate, instead identifying more closely with their mother country. This has resulted in the alienation of ethnic Russians in Estonia.

OTHER PEOPLES

Before Soviet rule, many people from neighboring countries lived in Estonia, such as Swedes, Germans, Latvians, and Finns. These people had historical and cultural links with Estonia and were generally part of a small, educated elite.

An Estonian rabbi holds the Torah during the inauguration ceremony of the Beit Bella synagogue in Tallinn.

Today's minorities are chiefly Slavic people who migrated from the former Soviet Union. Apart from Russians, there are significant numbers of Ukrainians and Belarusians in Estonia. Along with people from Azerbaijan, Armenia, Moldova, the Soviet Far East, and Siberia, these settlers were recruited by the government in Moscow to work in the construction, oil-shale, and power industries in the 1950s, 1960s, and 1970s. Separated from their homeland and discouraged from learning about Estonian culture, most non-Russians melted into the Russian-speaking population, learning Russian and sending their children to Russian-language schools. Consequently in postindependence Estonia these people had difficulties assimilating with native Estonians.

The other major ethnic groups in Estonia are Jews, Latvians, Poles, Germans, and Lithuanians. The Latvians live mainly in the rural areas near the Latvian border.

THE SETOS

The Setos are a small group of Finno-Ugric people who inhabit the Setumaa region of southeastern Estonia and the formerly disputed Russian area around the city of Pechory, southeast of Estonia. The Setos have ancient ethnic and traditional ties with Estonians. In the Middle Ages, the Setos came under the control of the Russian principality of Pskov, and the region has been occupied by Russian troops for most of the time since. Over the centuries the Setos drifted away from their Estonian counterparts and absorbed more Slavic culture and traditions, while Estonians were heavily influenced by German and Swedish culture. Most Setos are Russian Orthodox Christians and speak a dialect of the Võru tongue, common in southeastern Estonia.

In 1993 the Estonian government introduced the Law of Cultural Autonomy, giving all minorities the legal right to preserve and celebrate their identity, language, and culture. By 2007 more than 200 ethnic societies promoting minority people had been registered—many funded by the government. Many are housed in the Estonian Nationalities Club in Tallinn, where cultural promotion and social activities are given priority. Orchestras have been developed, and handicraft groups and choirs have been formed. The Slavic Cultural and Charity Society revived traditional Russian song and dance festivals.

FINNO-UGRIC PEOPLE   Finno-Ugric peoples such as the Mordvinians, Karelians, Udmurts, and Maris also moved to Estonia as part of Soviet migration policies in the 1960s and 1970s. They came from areas west of the Ural Mountains and near the Volga River in Russia and are related to the Estonians by ancient linguistic and ethnic ties. Today around 3,000 non-Estonian Finno-Ugric people live in Estonia.

ESTONIAN SWEDES   Estonian Swedes have traditionally lived along the northwest coast of the country, around Haapsalu and on the islands. Before the Soviet occupation, as many as 8,000 Swedes lived in Estonia. Most fled the advancing Russian army in 1944. Now there are only a few hundred Swedes in the country.

The Seto people have retained a unique style of folksinging. A lead singer improvises poetry that is repeated in complex harmonies by a group of five or six women, one of whom sings in a higher tone than the others.

LIFESTYLE

The youths of Estonia enjoying themselves
in one of Tallinn's many nightspots.

CHAPTER 7

O

F THE FORMER SOVIET COUNTRIES, Estonia has been one of the fastest to adapt to free-market economics. Today Estonia is fully integrated into the world economy, and Estonians enjoy the benefits, with one of the highest standards of living in Eastern Europe.

This was not always the case, however. In the immediate aftermath of independence, life was very hard for many Estonians, with the transition from a socialist, centrally controlled economy to a free-market economy and self-rule creating high unemployment, food and fuel shortages, poorer services, and general uncertainty.

Today the lifestyle of Estonians is very much influenced by the changing seasons, with indoor activities dominating during the long, dark, cold winters and outdoor festivals as the high points of the cultural calendar in the long, light days of summer. In recent years excellent outdoor sports and social facilities have been developed all over the country, and Estonians' rising living standard has allowed them to enjoy the fruits of their independence.

CITY LIFE

More than 70 percent of Estonians live in towns or cities. The center of Tallinn is still a pleasant place to live, with historic architecture, picturesque towers,

Estonians are often seen using their cell phones and laptops.

and cobbled streets. The number of places to eat and drink in Tallinn has greatly increased since the Soviet era, when restaurants were few and service generally poor. Now most streets in the capital have a place to eat or drink. Cellar bars and cafés are very popular in urban areas, providing warm and cozy retreats from the winter weather. However, they are considered too hot and stuffy in summer, when Estonians prefer to be outdoors, in the countryside if possible. Nightclubs are also popular in Tallinn.

The goods in Estonian shops compare favorably with those available elsewhere in Europe and include chic fashions, especially in Tallinn. The Scandinavian influence is apparent in the type of clothing found in stores in the capital. Western-style boutiques and barbershops are also increasingly common.

A new housing culture has developed in the past 10 years, and many Estonians live in houses or newly built apartments of sophisticated, cutting-edge design. Estonia's newfound prosperity has led people to spend a lot of time and money improving their homes to make them more attractive and more comfortable.

The Viru shopping center lies in the downtown district of Tallinn.

Tenement blocks still ring many of Estonia's major cities, however, a leftover from the Soviet era. Tallinn's Old Town seems a world away from the drab housing developments of Õisemäe and Mustamäe south of the city. Many of Estonia's Russian minority live in these high-rise suburbs. Overcrowding is a problem, with parents plus two children often squeezed into a one-bedroom apartment. Electricity and water supplies are often unreliable. There is still high unemployment in some urban areas, especially in Narva, Kohtla-Järve, and Sillamäe. The living standard in these cities is poor because of the horrendous pollution that characterizes the northeast of the country and causes health problems, especially lung and heart disease.

COUNTRY LIFE

Nearly a third of Estonia's population live in the rural areas, almost all of them ethnic Estonians. Estonians feel themselves to be essentially country people. Following independence, many rural Estonians wished to return to the prewar idyll of the self-sufficient smallholder. The state-run collective farms were swiftly replaced by family-run farms that blossomed in the hands of their new owners.

Rural Estonians working on their farm near Põltsamaa.

Many city dwellers have summerhouses in the country, or at least an allotment of land on the outskirts of their city. Estonians' strong identification with nature and love of solitude take them to their country cottages every summer in search of rural tranquility. Gardening is popular, and many people take great pride in their gardens.

Children feeding pigeons in Kadriorg Park in Tallinn.

Rural Estonians are far more traditional and less exposed to outside influences—not many speak a foreign language apart from Russian. Creature comforts are fewer in the country. People put in long, hard hours of manual labor and suffer the physical privations that come with long, cold, and dark winters. Some houses do not have running hot water or central heating, and wood is often stacked in neat piles around the house for fuel. Off the main highways, unpaved, dusty country roads lack proper markings or signs. Unlike in the cities, shops, businesses, and restaurants tend to close at 5 P.M., and everything is closed on Sunday. These inconveniences are offset by the advantages of breathing clean air, having plenty of space, and being able to indulge in picking wildflowers, berries, and mushrooms.

FAMILY AND MARRIAGE

The typical Estonian family is the small nuclear family, consisting of a mother, a father, and two children. It is rare for older relatives to live in the same house as their children and grandchildren. Estonians have developed a liberal, easygoing attitude toward sex and marriage. More than half of the children are born out of wedlock. Estonia's birthrate has remained low for

No matter how small and simple the country house, it generally has a sauna. Estonians are fond of relaxing in a hot and steamy sauna, especially in winter.

some years, with an average of approximately 10 children per 1,000 people being born every year since 2003. In 2006 the fertility rate was 1.4 children per female. In the Soviet era, the population increased mainly because of the arrival of immigrants from other parts of the Soviet Union. With immigration halted since independence, the population has been steadily declining. Abortion is common, with the number of abortions each year outpacing the number of births. Child care and child rearing have become expensive in recent years, so couples prefer to raise a small family so that they can maintain their standard of living.

Although the marriage rate is low in Estonia, in recent years there has been an increase in the number of people marrying. More than half of couples live together before getting married, and many continue to cohabit without marrying. Divorce is increasingly common. This has led to quite a diversity of lifestyles in Estonia, with both the traditional extended family and the two-parent family being less common than in the past. Whereas in Latvia marriages between ethnic Latvians and minorities are common, in Estonia marriages between ethnic Estonians and Russians and other minorities are comparatively rare.

Traditional marriage practices have also become less common in Estonia. This is partly a result of 50 years of Soviet policies and partly because very few modern Estonians are religious.

A typical family unit in Estonia.

HOSPITALITY

Estonians are not known for their outward friendliness, and unlike Lithuanians and Latvians, they do not invite people they barely know to their homes. Estonians are not selfish or unfriendly, but they value friendship highly and do not offer invitations lightly.

Estonians normally greet each other with a handshake, and some men may tip their hats. Bringing cut flowers when visiting is universal for any kind

An elderly couple
enjoying a walk.

of gathering, celebration, or party, and they always prove a popular gift. Flower shops are found on nearly every street corner in towns and cities.

When Estonians entertain at home, it is usually to share a meal and drinks with family and close friends. Estonians are at their most relaxed when gathered around a table. Alcohol often features prominently. Drinking alcohol is a popular way of relaxing in Estonia, as it is throughout Scandinavia and the other Baltic states. Cheap alcohol is one of the primary reasons many Finns visit Tallinn for day or weekend trips.

AN AGING POPULATION

Life expectancy is 67 years for Estonian men and 78 years for Estonian women. This has changed very little since the 1960s. A high proportion of ethnic Estonians—one in six—is over 65 years old, and trends suggest that Estonia will support an increasingly elderly population. Before independence, young immigrants arrived from other parts of the Soviet Union. As a result, there is a greater proportion of young people among the ethnic minorities than among the rest of the population. The low fertility rates have also contributed to a disproportionately aging population.

In the past, not enough attention was paid to providing housing and services for the older generation. Now the government has had to invest in housing, social services, medical care, and transportation for this group. This need has placed severe demands on a developing and overstretched economy.

EDUCATION

Today the aim of the education system is to promote Estonian language and culture and teach computer literacy and foreign languages. Most schools are run by the state, though private schools are slowly being introduced. According to the constitution, education is compulsory for all children from ages seven to 17. In 2005 there were 625 primary and secondary schools in Estonia. Higher education normally lasts for five or six years and is based on a credit system, in which students must gain a certain number of credits to complete their degree. Education in Estonia is based around the state curriculum, which is compulsory for all schools, whether state run or private.

The University of Tartu, Estonia's oldest university, was established by King Gustavus Adolphus of Sweden in 1632. The language of instruction was Swedish, later to be replaced by first German and then Russian in the 1880s. Estonian was introduced as the language of instruction in 1919. It is estimated that one fifth of the population of Tartu is either studying or working at the university.

Founded in 1938, the Estonian Academy of Sciences is Estonia's national academy of science.

ELEMENTARY AND SECONDARY SCHOOLS It is compulsory for children to attend elementary and secondary school, beginning at age seven. Students are obliged to stay in school until they have completed their basic education

The magnificent Tartu University is a sight to behold at night.

At the University of Tartu there is a famous sacrificial stone where students, having adapted a pagan custom, ritually burn their notebooks at midnight on the Thursday before their exams.

or are 17. Most students graduate to a higher level of secondary education, called upper secondary schools, similar to American high schools. A smaller percentage—roughly one quarter—go on to vocational schools that teach skills designed to prepare them for the workplace.

The constitution requires that lessons are taught in Estonian, although local schools can decide to use other languages as well if the majority of students are non-Estonian speakers. For example, in schools where most students are Russian speakers, it is quite common for lessons to be taught in Russian. Students are also required to learn at least two foreign languages. The most popular choices are English, German, Russian, Finnish, and French.

COLLEGES College education generally lasts five or six years. In 2005, 67,000 Estonian students went into higher education to gain degrees and professional qualifications. The largest public universities are the University of Tartu, the Tallinn University of Technology, the Estonian Academy of Arts, the Estonian Academy of Music, the Estonian University of Life Sciences (formerly the Estonian Agricultural University), and Tallinn University. The Estonian Business School is the country's largest private university.

The University of Tartu is Estonia's oldest and biggest university, with more than 17,000 students. It has Estonia's largest library, which owns the first book written in Estonian—a prayer book published in 1525. Most college courses are taught in Estonian, and students who wish to continue

In 2006, according to Statistics Estonia, 11 percent of female and 4 percent of male employees were working part-time, compared with 4 percent of women and less than 2 percent of men in 1989. The popularity of part-time work has grown more rapidly among women.

A pharmacy in Estonia.

WOMEN AT WORK

In general women have adapted more easily to changes in lifestyle and work in postindependence Estonia than men. Women have found it easier to develop the skills needed in the new workplace, such as dealing graciously with strangers. However, there is still considerable institutionalized inequality. Although Estonian women are legally entitled to equal pay at work, in reality they are often paid less despite having on average more education than their male counterparts. Traditional thinking that regards men as the chief breadwinners still dominates in Estonia, though women make up more than half of the working population. In addition, Estonian women tend to work in traditionally female professions, such as teaching, health care, and dentistry. For example, they make up the majority of secondary-school teachers, and there are only 18 women in the 101-seat Riigikogu. Women also do most of the household chores and look after the children despite their work commitments.

their education in Russian generally complete their studies in Russia. There are a number of private institutions, including the American-run Concordia International University in Tallinn, where the syllabus concentrates on practical subjects such as business studies and communications, and classes are taught in English.

WELFARE AND HEALTH CARE

When Estonia was still a part of the Soviet Union, health care and welfare were provided and funded by the state. This system has gradually been restructured during the past 15 years with the introduction of pension and unemployment plans. In 1994 a minimum income was guaranteed to all Estonian families. The recent recession has meant that an increasing amount of government taxes is spent on unemployment benefit, with unemployment running at 5.2 percent in 2007 and 5.1 percent in 2008.

Free medical care is provided for all school-age children. Estonia's publicly run hospitals have gradually improved since independence, though financial constraints have slowed this progress. A system of medical insurance has been introduced, and medical care is free for all residents.

RELIGION

The interior of Saint Olaf's Church in Tallinn.

CHAPTER 8

A T THE MERCY OF SHIFTING SPHERES of influence, Estonia has been left with a legacy of churches and faiths, consisting of Lutheranism, Catholicism, Orthodoxy, Judaism, and Islam.

For nearly 500 years Lutheranism, a Protestant religion, has been Estonia's official faith. Despite a nominal adherence to the Lutheran Church, Estonians are (and have long been) one of the most secular people in Europe. Today only 29 percent of Estonians claim to have any religious conviction (though the figure is higher among ethnic Russians, who tend to follow the Orthodox faith).

The government has associated itself with the Estonian Evangelical Lutheran Church as part of its nation-building program, and religious studies have been reintroduced into the public school curriculum. Historically there has been considerable tolerance of other faiths, and freedom of religious practice and belief is guaranteed under the constitution.

A sketch depicting Martin Luther delivering a sermon in the 16th century.

Members of the ancient Russian Orthodox sect the Old Believers have lived on the shores of Lake Peipsi since the 18th century. The first members came to Estonia to avoid persecution under Czar Peter the Great. They reject traditional Orthodox leadership and conduct church services in Old Church Slavonic, a medieval language.

ANCIENT PRACTICES

Estonians' ancient cosmogony is still preserved in folkloric traditions. Before the forced conversion of Estonians to Christianity by the German crusaders, animistic beliefs held sway along the Baltic coast. Trees, rocks, hills, fields, and animals were worshiped as powerful spiritual forces. Much of this pagan religion was a product of the lifestyle of a hunter-fisher society at a time when trees covered most of Estonia.

Forests were thought to contain powerful spirits that could cause those who had behaved badly—especially those who damaged the forest—to lose their way or be attacked by forest animals. Springs, rivers, and lakes were also believed to contain spirits that could injure or kill the unwary. Spirits could be both protective and dangerous forces. The dead were also thought to inhabit the world as spirits and could be called on for assistance through funeral rites and sacrifices.

A stone beach on the coast of Saaremaa Island. Old animist beliefs may have faded away, but a respect and love of nature remains deeply embedded in the Estonian psyche.

SACRED TREES

As a result of ancient Estonian religious practices and the people's love of nature, there are many sacred trees in Estonia today. In ancient times, Estonians would gather under oak trees before making important decisions. Estonia's most famous sacred tree, the Pühajärv Oak, decorates the country's two-kroon banknote. Standing 65 feet (20 m) tall between a cow pasture and a lake, the Pühajärv Oak is believed to be the oldest and biggest oak in the country. In 1841 this famous tree became the site of unrest when peasants fought their German landlords over harsh and exploitative working conditions.

THE EVANGELICAL LUTHERAN CHURCH

Lutheranism—the dominant religion of most of Scandinavia and northern Germany—has been Estonia's official religion since it replaced Catholicism following the Reformation in 1520. Because of continuing warfare, however, the Lutheran Church developed slowly in Estonia, remaining a superficial influence until the establishment of a state church by Swedish rulers in the 17th century. Estonians were unable to gain direct access to the teachings of the church until an Estonian edition of the New Testament was published in 1686, making religion more accessible to the common people. In the early 1700s, the Moravian Brethren arrived in Estonia to begin a popular lay-Christian movement. The Brethren were suppressed by the Lutheran Church, but they left a lasting tradition of informal home schooling and literacy. A full translation of the Bible was written in 1739, and religion was taught in newly established schools.

Estonia's first churches were built on the islands in the early 13th century, following the conquest by the German crusaders. They were simple structures and were used chiefly for defense. Many of Estonia's pre-Reformation churches were decorated by local and foreign artists.

Lutheran practices suffered during the Czarist years because of the state's overt promotion of the Orthodox Church. But in 1919 the church was reorganized and renamed the Estonian Evangelical Lutheran Church, for the first time coming under Estonian control. In Estonia's first period of independence (1920—40), the Lutheran Church flourished, and 80 percent of the population were officially listed as members. Following the Soviet occupation in 1945, religious worshipers were persecuted by the atheist Communist state. It was not officially a crime to be a religious believer, but it was against the law to teach religion to children. Two-thirds of Estonia's clergy disappeared in the early years of Soviet rule, and many churches were confiscated or closed down. By the 1970s fewer than 10 percent of Estonians, many of them Baptists, were prepared to publicly claim adherence to Christianity. In the late 1980s, as part of the liberating effect of glasnost, the religious repression lifted. There was a surge of interest in the Lutheran Church. The church allied itself to the burgeoning independence movement, and Estonians wanted to express their newfound freedom by celebrating everything Estonian. The number of baptisms rose tenfold, although this initial enthusiasm quickly waned. There are approximately 165 Lutheran congregations in the country today with approximately 180,000 members.

Lutheran practice is far more austere than that of the Catholic and Orthodox faiths. The preaching of sermons plays an essential role in the service, as does the singing of hymns. Lutherans observe just two sacraments: Baptism and the Lord's Supper, or Holy Communion. Church rites include confirmation, ordination, marriage, and burial. Confirmation is normally given between the ages of 10 and 15 and includes Baptism and public profession of the faith by the recipient.

THE ORTHODOX CHURCH

The Russian Orthodox Church was officially established in the 18th century following Estonia's absorption into Czarist Russia. Promoted by the Russian bureaucracy, Orthodoxy had moderate success, due in part to the peasants' desire to find an alternative to Lutheranism, perceived to be the religion of the German landlords. In the 19th century Orthodox membership rose as high as 20 percent. Czar Alexander III commissioned the construction of Orthodox churches throughout Estonia. The Alexander Nevsky Cathedral, built in the 1890s, is the most famous of these and stands on Toompea Hill in the center of Tallinn. Since independence, the status of the Orthodox Church has been a source of friction between Russia and Estonia, as well as within the ethnic Russian and Estonian Orthodox congregations in Estonia. In the early 1990s, negotiations were held between the

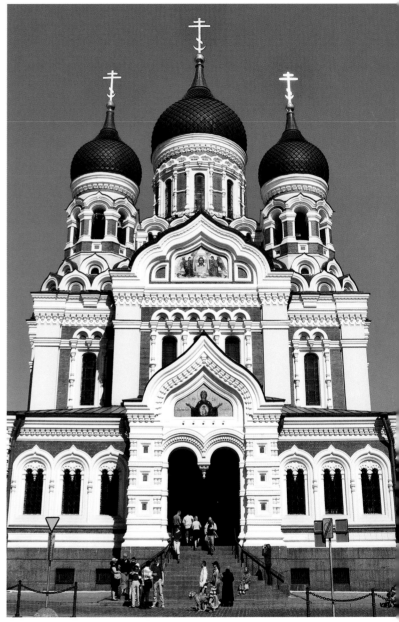

The beautifully crafted Alexander Nevsky Cathedral.

Constantinople and Moscow Patriarchs over the status of Estonia's Orthodox communities, many of which wanted to return to Constantinople's jurisdiction. In 1996 the Constantinople Patriarch decided to restore the Estonian Orthodox Church to its jurisdiction, much against the Moscow authorities' wishes. Orthodox Estonians were allowed to choose whether they wanted to continue with the Moscow-centered faith or become a part of the church under Constantinople jurisdiction.

Today the Estonian Orthodox Church, which has a mainly ethnic Russian congregation and is subordinate to the Moscow Patriarchate, has 30 congregations with an estimated 170,000 members, while the Estonian Apostolic Orthodox Church, which is an autonomous church subordinate to Constantinople, has 61 congregations with roughly 25,000 members. The current primate of the Estonian Apostolic Orthodox Church is Stephanos, Metropolitan of Tallinn and all Estonia, elected in 1999.

Ritual is an important part of worship for the Russian Orthodox Church and includes music, the burning of incense, and chanting. Icons are positioned around the inside of most churches, and walls are covered with frescoes depicting religious events and symbolizing religious ideas. Believers pray in front of the icons, lighting candles as offerings and often kissing the icons as a sign of respect and supplication. The experience is intended to convey the mysterious essence of the faith. In contrast, the Estonian Orthodox Church is more austere in character, and its services and churches lack the colorful decoration and pageantry of their Russian counterparts.

The Pühtitsa nunnery in Kuremäe is a Russian Orthodox convent that was established in 1891.

OTHER CHRISTIAN CHURCHES

Other Christian religions, such as the Baptists, the Methodists, and the Seventh-day Adventists, have been growing in popularity in Estonia. There are an estimated 6,000 practicing Catholics in Estonia, many of whom come from Estonia's Polish, Ukrainian, and Lithuanian minorities. The Baptist and Methodist Churches have proved popular with some Estonians, who have sought new forms of Christian worship outside the Lutheran and Orthodox faiths. Jehovah's Witness and Mormon congregations also flourish.

OTHER RELIGIONS

Many non-Christian religions are practiced in Estonia today, chiefly by ethnic minorities who came to Estonia during the Soviet period. Additionally, the more mystical elements of traditional Estonian religion have contributed to the rising popularity of holistic beliefs such as the Hare Krishna movement.

A 16th-century Catholic church in Tallinn Old Town.

JUDAISM Before World War II, about 4,000 Jews lived in Estonia. Many of them escaped to Russia before the Nazi occupation, when the remaining 1,000 Jews were murdered, and the Nazi officials triumphantly declared Estonia to be *Judenfrei* (free of Jews). Since World War II, a small Jewish population has reestablished itself. There are approximately 2,500 Jews living in Estonia today, mainly in and around Tallinn, where there is a synagogue.

ISLAM Estonia has very few Muslims; most arrived in the country to work on industrial projects during the Soviet period. Estonia's Muslims are mainly from the former Soviet republics of the Caucasus region and Central Asia and include Azerbaijanis, Ossetians, and Uzbeks.

LANGUAGE

A man talks on a pay phone along the street.

CHAPTER 9

ESTONIAN IS THE NATIONAL language of Estonia and is spoken as the mother tongue by almost all ethnic Estonians. Russian, Ukrainian, Belarusian, and Finnish are also widely spoken by the larger ethnic minorities in Estonia, while to a much smaller degree, German, Latvian, Lithuanian, Polish, Swedish, and Tatar are also spoken.

Since independence, language has become a highly politicized issue in Estonia. All citizens are required to speak the national language to a minimal level, regardless of their mother tongue. Consequently Estonian has been introduced as the primary means of instruction in schools, mainly with the long-term aim of integrating non-Estonians into society. However, the government passed a law that permits local government administrative procedures in districts with a non-Estonian majority to be conducted in a minority language. In practice, this means Russian in much of the northeast of the country but Estonian almost everywhere else.

Old ship signs in an Estonian museum.

Women having a conversation outside Kadriorg Palace in Tallinn.

ESTONIAN

Estonian is the native language of almost one million people in Estonia today and is spoken to varying degrees of fluency by people of Estonian descent in Sweden, Germany, the United States, Canada, and Britain. Estonian belongs to the Finno-Ugric family of languages, as do Hungarian, Finnish, and the languages of the Sami (sometimes called Lapps) in northern Scandinavia, the Livs in Latvia, and the Mari, the Khanti, the Mansi, and the Mordvins in the Russian Federation. It is most closely related to Finnish, and Estonians and Finns have little trouble understanding each other.

A considerable amount of German vocabulary has become part of the Estonian language over the years. However, much of the German influence was "Estonianized" when the country became independent in 1919.

Johannes Aavik (1880—1973) is credited with introducing some important linguistic innovations, including expanding the Estonian vocabulary to include

The percentage of ethnic Russians speaking Estonian has increased from 15 percent in 1991 to 40 percent today. Among 18- to 24-year-old Russians, that figure is nearly 60 percent.

a number of Finnish words that offer greater flexibility. Finnish "loan words" have easily been incorporated into the language. In recent years many English words have also become common.

Early written Estonian was strongly Germanic in character. The first text to appear in the Estonian language was a translation of the Lutheran catechism in 1535. A New Testament in the southern Estonian dialect did not appear until 1680, and a northern version was not published until 1715. Using the northern dialect as a basis, Anton Thor Helle united the two dialects and translated the Bible in 1739. Käsu Hans wrote the first known example of secular Estonian literature, a poem in which he lamented the destruction of Tartu in the Great Northern War, in 1708. The language developed more fully with the flowering of an Estonian literary movement in the 19th century, which included the first native Estonian poet, Kristjan Jaak Peterson. Friedrich Kreutzwald's epic compilation, *Kalevipoeg*, established an authentic Estonian literary tradition, of which the poet Lydia Koidula was one of the greatest examples.

The Estonian alphabet is based on the Latin alphabet. It has 23 letters, plus nine foreign letters that have been borrowed for use from the many foreign words that have been adopted into Estonian over the years.

"Cannot the tongue of this land In the fire of incantation Rising up to the heavens Seek for eternity?" –Kristjan Jaak Peterson, writing in 1821 of the rebirth of the Estonian language.

A street sign in Tallinn Old Town.

Estonian is considered one of the most beautiful languages in the world, perhaps because of its numerous elongated vowels and few harsh consonants.

a	ah *as in* "father"		r	*the r is rolled*
b	*voiceless, similar to the p in* "copy"		s	*like the English s but voiceless and weaker*
(c)			š	sh *as in* "shoe"—*appears only in foreign words*
d	*voiceless, similar to the t in* "city"			
e	a *as in* "hay"		z	s *as in* "is"
(f)			ž	s *as in* "pleasure"—*used only in foreign words*
g	*voiceless, similar to the ck in* "ticket"			
h	h *as in* "house"		t	t *as in* "tall"
i	ee *as in* "feet"		u	oo *as in* "boot"
j	y *as in* "yes"		v	v *as in* "violet"
k	k *as in* "kitchen"		(w)	
l	l *as in* "lily"		õ	ir *as in* "girl"
m	m *as in* "mother"		ä	a *as in* "cat"
n	n *as in* "not"		ö	u *as in* "fur" *but with rounded lips*
o	o *as in* "hope"		ü	oo *as in* "boot"
p	p *as in* "pot"		(x)	
(q)			(y)	

Estonian has a reputation for being a difficult language to master. The main challenge is vocabulary, because Finno-Ugric languages have very few word roots in common with Indo-European languages. There are 14 cases for each noun, while grammatical categories are usually marked by suffixes added to the stem of the noun or the verb. Verb endings, in contrast, follow very simple patterns, and there are no articles or genders. Similar to English, Estonian is an idiomatic language. For a country whose national identity is

Opposite: A stone plaque announcing the house of the Estonian Literary Society in Tallinn.

In Estonian, double vowels elongate the regular vowel sound. Estonian is also famous for its unusual contrast of three degrees of consonant and vowel length. For example, koli (KO-li, "junk") is pronounced with a short o sound, while kooli (KOH-li, "of school") uses a longer o, and kooli (KOO-li, "to school") an extralong o.

aa   a *as in "father"*

ee   eh *as in the interjection "eh?"*

ii   ee *as in "feel"*

oo   eau *as in "bureau"*

uu   oo *as in "food"*

ää   *same as ä but with a more open mouth*

öö   *same as ö but longer and higher*

õõ   *same as õ but longer*

üü   *same as ü but longer and clearer*

so closely associated with the land, it is not surprising to find Estonian surnames such as Meri (Sea), Kask (Birch tree) Ilves (Lynx), Maasikas (Strawberry), and Rohumaa (Grassland).

ESTONIAN DIALECTS   Estonian has two major dialects: a Tallinn-based northern dialect and a more rural southern dialect. Recently linguists have divided Estonian into eight subdialects: northeastern coastal, central, insular (island), eastern, and western, plus three main dialects of the south: Mulgi, Tartu, and Võru.

ESTONIAN SWEDISH   Estonian Swedish belongs to the eastern group of dialects of the Swedish language. Isolated from the mother tongue, Estonian Swedish has many archaic characteristics and is not

easily understood by modern Swedes. There are only about 100 people in Estonia who can speak Estonian Swedish. Ordinary Swedish is popular for cultural and business reasons.

OTHER LANGUAGES

English, German, and French are becoming increasingly popular. English and German are widely spoken in the tourist areas of Tallinn and Tartu. English is fast becoming a lingua franca among young people.

FINNISH Finnish is spoken in much of northern Estonia: it is estimated that at least 5,000 people speak it as their mother tongue, while many more speak it as a second language. Because of its similarity to Estonian, people of Tallinn in particular speak some Finnish because of the regular flow of Finnish tourists and businesspeople from Helsinki.

RUSSIAN Russian is a familiar language in Estonia. Until independence, many Estonians were required to speak Russian in order to communicate with the authorities. Consequently many Estonians are fluent in Russian, even if they rarely speak it.

A typical parking sign in Estonia.

NEWSPAPERS AND PUBLICATIONS

Given its small population, the number and range of newspapers and magazines in Estonia is quite remarkable, with titles covering every conceivable subject. Seventy percent of all publications are published in Estonian. The main national Estonian-language newspapers include *Eesti Ekspress* (*Estonian Express*), *Eesti Päevaleht* (*Estonian Daily*), and *Postimees*

(*The Postman*), which is Estonia's oldest newspaper and has been published in Tartu since 1857. *Postimees* and other newspapers also have Russian-language editions, but the most popular Russian-language daily is *Molodezh Estonii*. Estonian law guarantees freedom of press, and local newspapers have been critical of the government. Foreign newspapers and magazines are also widely available. In addition, Estonia has a number of good quality Internet news services in Estonian, English, and Russian.

TELEVISION

Television broadcasting improved greatly after independence, especially with the appearance of independent operators and foreign programming. There are several major independent television channels, as well as the state-run Eesti Televisioon (Estonian Television). The latter, which broadcasts programs in both Estonian and Russian, has a reputation for being dull and unimaginative. State-run broadcast media continue to receive government subsidies. Tallinn Commercial Television operates one channel that broadcasts in Estonian and Russian. Other commercial channels include Kanal 2, which broadcasts classic Estonian and Hollywood movies, and TV3, which offers American programming with Estonian subtitles. Cable television is widely available and offers programs in English, Russian, German, and Finnish.

For many years, people living in the north of the country have been able to watch Finnish television—in Tallinn as many as four Finnish stations are available. In the Soviet era, Finnish television offered Estonians a window on the Western world and a glimpse of another lifestyle.

A newsstand displaying the various newspapers available. A few English-language papers are published in Estonia, including *The Baltic Times* and Tallinn's *The City Paper*, which offers helpful information to visitors.

ARTS

The stunning Kumu Art Museum by architect
Pekka Vapaavuori stands in Tallinn.

UNTIL THE 19TH CENTURY, traditional Estonian culture existed mainly in the form of peasant folktales and verses, passed down through the ages by word of mouth. Folk poetry proved a resilient and important force in maintaining Estonian identity, helping Estonians retain a sense of their culture despite many centuries of foreign occupation.

Estonia's national awakening in the late 19th century was centered around a development and exploration of the country's folklore and folk traditions, providing the basis for a separate Estonian culture and thriving literary, musical, and artistic movements.

Since independence, Estonia's artistic heritage has played an important part in rebuilding people's sense of national identity. The Estonian Heritage Society was created in 1987 with the mandate of preserving and promoting the artistic and historical culture of Estonia, and to date, it has been very successful.

Miniatures of Estonia's numerous architectural delights in a souvenir shop in Tallinn.

MUSIC AND SINGING

The earliest mention of Estonian singing dates back to *Gesta Danorum* (*Deeds of the Danes*) by 12th-century author Saxo Grammaticus. Saxo speaks of Estonian warriors who sang at night while waiting to go into battle.

Music and singing are Estonia's most important and popular forms of artistic expression. The origins of folk singing in Estonia go back at least to the first millennium B.C. as runic verse—short tunes with a limited range of notes but rich in variation. These songs were accompanied by traditional instruments, such as the *kannel* (KUHN-ehl), a kind of zither, along with whistles, pipes, flutes, and fiddles. Rhyming folk songs did not appear until the 18th century, when the Moravian Brethren congregations sang chorales in four-part harmony. The first Estonian arrangements of choir music were created in the mid-19th century.

Estonia's first symphony orchestra was founded in 1900 in Tartu. Rudolf Tobias (1873—1918) wrote the first Estonian symphonic work, the overture *Julius Caesar*, in 1896 and followed this with Estonia's first piano concerto (1897) and oratorio (1909). Estonian symphonic music reached its peak in the country's first period of independence between 1920 and 1940. Estonia's first significant opera, *Vikerlased* (*The Vikings*), was written by Evald Aav (1900—39). Eduard Tubin (1905—82) wrote the first Estonian ballet, *Kratt* (*The Goblin*), in 1943. He fled to Sweden at the end of World War II to escape persecution under the Soviet occupation.

Musicians dressed in traditional Estonian outfits in the historic center of Tallinn.

Estonian composer Arvo Pärt receiving the Leonie Sonning Music Prize.

Most recently Veljo Tormis (b. 1930) has revived ancient forms of runic chanting and uses them in his choral works. His best-known works, which are notoriously difficult to perform, are *Raua needmine* (*Curse upon Iron*) and *Ingerimaa õhtud* (*Ingrian Evenings*), both part of a cycle of songs. Currently Arvo Pärt (b. 1935) is Estonia's most widely acclaimed international composer, famous for his minimalist style and choral compositions. His best-known choral works are *Tabula Rasa*, *Saint John's Passion*, *Cantus in Memoriam*, *Benjamin Britten*, and *Fratres*.

From October to April, classical performances are held almost every night at Tallinn's Estonian National Opera. In addition to housing the national opera company, it is home to the Estonian National Symphony Orchestra and stages musicals and ballets. Performances are given by the Symphony Orchestra or the Philharmonic Chamber Orchestra and Choir. The latter's recording of Pärt's *Te Deum* was nominated for a Grammy Award. Small ensembles and solo performers also play in smaller halls and theaters in Tallinn, Tartu, and Pärnu.

Popular music, probably Estonia's most rapidly expanding art form, plays a major role in Estonia's celebrated summer music festivals. Both foreign and local rock, rhythm and blues, soul, and jazz bands have a wide following. The composer Alo Mattiisen is known for using Estonian folk chants in some of his songs. Few Estonian pop singers have succeeded internationally, although duo Tanel Padar and Dave Benton did win the Eurovision Song Contest in 2001. Rock music is still associated with the "singing revolution" of the late 1980s, a gesture of defiance that the Estonian people will remember proudly for generations.

The All-Estonian Song Celebration (Laulupidu) takes place in Tallinn's Song Celebration Grounds every five years in July. The first festival took place in Tartu in 1869. Choirs throughout the country compete to participate in the festival, to combine into a single choir of about 20,000 singers. The most recent festival was held in 2009, and the next festival will be in 2014.

LITERATURE

Because Estonia experienced a long period of foreign domination, an Estonian-language literature developed quite late—in the middle of the 19th century, at the time of Estonia's national awakening. Kristjan Jaak Peterson (1801—22) is considered Estonia's first original poet. Two men remembered for their contributions to early Estonian literature—Friedrich Faehlmann (1798—1850) and Friedrich Kreutzwald (1803—82)—were both doctors with a keen interest in Estonian folklore. Faehlmann collected verses of folk poetry from rural Estonia. After Faehlmann's untimely death, Kreutzwald continued his work. Between 1857 and 1861 Kreutzwald compiled and published Estonia's national epic, *Kalevipoeg* (*Son of Kalev*). The epic consists of 19,023 runic verses and tells the story of the mythical founder of the Estonian nation.

Postimees, Estonia's first Estonian-language newspaper, was founded in 1857 by Johann Jannsen (1819—90). It contributed significantly to the national awakening. Jannsen's daughter, Lydia,

Estonian author Jaan Kross.

There is a museum dedicated to the writer Eduard Vilde in the Kadriorg Park in Tallinn.

who wrote under the pen name Lydia Koidula (1843—86), produced some highly original and patriotic poetry. Many consider her collection of verse, *Emajõe ööbik* (*The Nightingale of Emajogi*), to be the most important literary work from Estonia's period of national awakening.

Toward the end of the 19th century, writing novels became more popular. Eduard Bornhöhe (1862—1923) wrote romantic novels. His novel *Tasuja* (*The Avenger*), written in 1880, commemorated Estonia's troubled past by depicting the struggle against the German crusaders. The most prominent writer in the realism genre was Eduard Vilde (1865—1933). His novel *Külmale maale* (*Banished*), written in 1896, is a stylistic landmark in Estonian fiction. In the historical trilogy *Mäeküla piimamees* (*Milkman of the Manor*), written in 1916, Vilde portrayed the inequalities of the Baltic—German feudal system. He also wrote plays, including *The Unattained Miracle* (1912) and *The Fire Dragon* (1913). His contemporary Juhan Liiv (1864—1913) was a poet and storywriter whose most notable works are *Ten Stories* (1893), *Vari* (*The Shadow*, 1894), and *Poems* (1909).

A group calling itself Noor-Eesti (Young Estonia) sought to create a modern, cosmopolitan Estonian literature. Chief among them were Gustav Suits (1883—1956), Friedebert Tuglas (1886—1971), and Johannes Aavik (1880—1973). During the independence era, Siuru, a literary group that took its name from a mythical songbird, shocked conventional taste by exploring sensual and erotic themes. Marie Under (1883—1980) was by far the most gifted member of this group, bursting on the scene with evocative, exciting, and emotional poetry of a power not previously experienced in Estonia. This period also produced Anton Hansen Tammsaare (1878—1940), considered to be Estonia's greatest novelist. His most impressive work, the five-volume *Tõde ja õigus* (*Truth and Justice*, 1926—33), explores Estonian social and political life from the 1870s to the 1920s.

Nobel Prize-nominated Estonian poet Jaan Kaplinski.

The Estonian folklorist Arvo Krikmann is internationally famous for his six-volume collection of Estonian proverbs, published both in print and online.

Jaan Kross (1920—2007) was probably Estonia's most famous contemporary writer, and many of his works have been translated into English. Kross was best known for *The Czar's Madman* (1978), a novel where he tackled contemporary Soviet issues through a historical theme. In 1998 he published *Treading Air*, a "fictional memoir" about his experiences during World War II. Kross was nominated several times for the Nobel Prize for Literature. Jaan Kaplinski (b. 1941) and Paul-Eerik Rummo (b. 1942) are Estonia's best-known modern poets. During the Soviet period, some of their poetry was censored by the government, but it circulated secretly in handwritten copies. Both Kross and Kaplinski were elected to the Riigikogu in the 1990s, while Rummo served as minister of culture and education from 1992 to 1994. Among other contemporary works, Mati Unt's *Things in the Night* (1990) and Tõnu Õnnepalu's *Border State* (1993) have been translated into numerous languages.

Theaters, such as this one in Tallinn, are very popular with Estonians.

THEATER

In recent years
Tallinn has become
the home of the
Jazzkaar jazz
festival. Every
April major names
in world jazz visit
Talinn to take part
in the 15-day jazz
marathon.

Theater is extremely popular in Estonia, and there are major theaters in Tallinn, Pärnu, Rakvere, Tartu, and Viljandi. Ten theaters are maintained by local governments. The oldest theater in Estonia is the Vanemuine, which was built in Tartu in 1870. Estonian drama was born of the same seeds as Estonian literature, springing from the period of national awakening at the end of the 19th century. Lydia Koidula's *Saaremaa onupoeg* (*The Cousin from Saaremaa*), written in 1870, was the first Estonian play to be staged.

In the Soviet era the theater, along with other institutions, was used by the Communist authorities for propaganda purposes and was heavily censored. The "thaw" following Stalin's death allowed the innovative theater enthusiast Voldemar Panso to found a drama school at the Tallinn Conservatoire in 1957. In 1965 he also founded the popular Youth Theater. The popular avant-garde movement was introduced in the 1960s by Evald Hermaküla and Jaan Tooming.

Today the most popular theater in the country is the Estonian Drama Theater in Tallinn, which developed in the 1950s. Many classic Western plays are popular and interpreted in an Estonian style. Plays are almost always performed in Estonian (sometimes with a Russian translation), except those of the Russian Drama Theater in Tallinn, which performs many classic 19th- and 20th-century Russian plays. Well-known actors include Ita Ever, Tiia Kriisa, Aarne Üksküla, Andrus Vaarik, and Tõnu Kark.

MOVIES

From the beginning of the Soviet occupation until the political thaw following Stalin's death, Estonian filmmaking consisted of documentaries and newsreels, mostly of a crudely political style. Movies with artistic merit did not begin to appear until the 1960s. Kaljo Kiisk's *Hullumeelsus* (*Lunacy*, 1968) was the first, and it tackled social issues. Leida Laius's *Naerata ometi* (*Smile Please*, 1985) and *Varastadud kohtumine* (*A Stolen Meeting*, 1988) also received international recognition. Peeter Simm has directed historical movies, including *Ideealmaastik* (*Ideal Landscape*, 1980) and *Inimene, keda polnud* (*The Man Who Never Was*, 1989). More recently, Elmo Nüganen's *Nimed marmortahvlil* (*Names in Marble*, 2002) was acclaimed for its realistic portrayal of Estonia's post-World War I struggle against the Bolsheviks, while Ilmar Raag's *Klass* (*The Class*, 2007) received critical recognition throughout Europe.

Above all else, Estonia has become famous for producing puppet and animated movies. Puppet moviemaking began in 1957 with Elbert Tuganov, who is perhaps best known for directing *Verine John* (*Bloody John*, 1974). Rein Raamat has achieved international success with his animated movies *Lend* (*The Flight*, 1973), *Suur Tõll* (*Tõll the Great*, 1980), and *Põrgu* (*Hell*, 1983). Priit Pärn has also received worldwide recognition for *Kolmnurk* (*The Triangle*, 1982), *Aeg maha* (*Time Out*, 1984), *Eine murul* (*Breakfast on the Grass*, 1987), and *Hotell E* (*Hotel E*, 1991) and for a recent television cartoon series for adults, *Frank and Wendy* (2005). Today experimental animators such as Mait Laas are gaining recognition for their surreal work, and cartoons such as *Leiutajateküla Lotte* (*Lotte from Inventorville*) have gained critical acclaim at film festivals in Europe and beyond.

A wealth of Estonian folklore from ancient times has been kept alive through the centuries in an oral tradition. These stories—passed down from generation to generation—provided the fledgling Estonian literary movement with material and a sense of tradition. More than a million pages of folk poetry are preserved in the national archives in Tartu.

A sculpture outside the Tallinn Art Hall.

VISUAL ARTS

Estonia's first art school was opened at Tartu University in 1803, but Estonian national art did not really take off until the period of national awakening. In 1906 the first general exhibition of Estonian art was held in Tartu.

Following Estonia's first period of independence, Estonian art split into a plethora of schools, including cubism, abstract expressionism, and neo-impressionism. During World War II and the Soviet occupation, many Estonian artists fled to the West. In the 1960s, following Stalin's death, art again began to develop. By the 1970s there were a profusion of artists and a thriving art scene in Estonia. Despite Soviet attempts to force Estonian art into the straitjacket of social realism, Estonian artists maintained their connection with European traditions. One of Estonia's best-known artists, Adamson-Eric (1902—68), was famous for figurative painting and abstract design for ceramics and bookbinding. Other artists include surrealist Eduard Wiiralt (1898—1954), famed for his woodcuts, etchings, and book illustrations, and Kaljo Põllu (b. 1934), who is internationally recognized for his graphic art.

ARCHITECTURE

Estonia's architectural heritage is dominated by the Gothic style of the Germans and the Swedes, who ruled the country from the 13th to the 18th centuries and built many of its castles and fortifications.

Tallinn is one of the most architecturally diverse cities in the Baltic region and has some well-preserved medieval buildings in a predominantly German style. The city walls date from the 14th to the 16th centuries. Most of the guildhalls, churches, and residences in the Old Town and Toompea also date from this period. The best example of Renaissance architecture

The Ammende Villa with its art nouveau style of architecture.

is the Blackhead's Fraternity Building in Tallinn, built in 1597, complete with intricately carved facade and portico. The baroque style of architecture, dating from the 17th and 18th centuries, can be seen in Narva's restored Town Hall, originally built in 1671. Czarist Russian rule brought a more classical style of architecture to Estonia. Many of the manor houses that have survived in Estonia were built in this period, as were the main buildings of Tartu University and Tartu Town Hall. Nineteenth-century architecture was dominated by Baltic-German architects trained in Riga and Saint Petersburg.

By the 1920s architects were trained for the first time in Tallinn itself. The art nouveau style became popular, exemplified by the Parliament Building in Tallinn, built in 1922. A more functional style dominated in the 1930s. Examples of this style are the Tallinn Art House and the Pärnu Beach Hotel. In the Soviet period, emphasis was placed on cheap, practical, industrial housing. Many of these prefab monstrosities can be seen on the edges of towns and cities, especially in the northeast and around Tallinn.

Estonia has some simple but impressive early churches, including the 13th-century Karja Church on Saaremaa Island and the ruined Jaani Church in Tartu. The Karja Church has many marvelous sculptures of 13th-century village life.

LEISURE

Pärnu Beach in Estonia. The locals enjoy going to the sandy beaches for a day of family fun.

CHAPTER 11

ESTONIANS' LEISURE ACTIVITIES are limited by both the country's geography and its climate. In summer, people like to go to the country or the coast and enjoy the outdoors while the weather is warm. In winter, indoor activities such as watching television, playing computer games, surfing the Internet, reading, and playing chess are popular.

Estonians are generally well read, and their interest in chess gained the country recognition internationally. Its best-known player, Paul Keres (1916—75) was nicknamed the Crown Prince of Chess.

Chess is a favorite national pastime, as demonstrated by Carmen Kass (right), top model and chairman of the Estonian Chess Association.

The Estonian government is keen to encourage its people to become Internet savvy, and there are 500 public Internet access points in the country, making Estonia the European country with the best coverage..

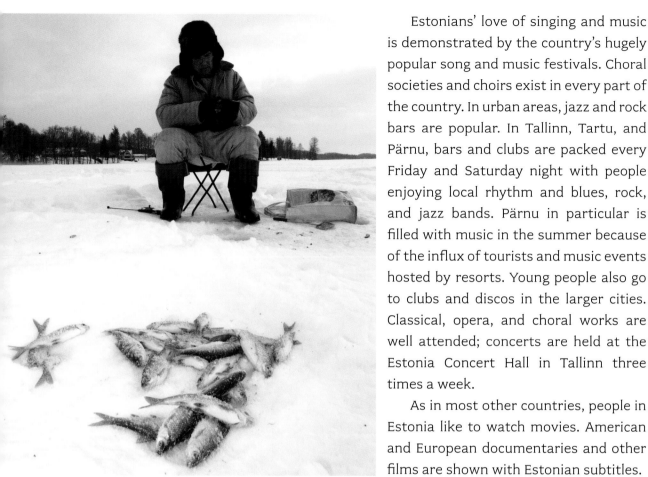

Estonians' love of singing and music is demonstrated by the country's hugely popular song and music festivals. Choral societies and choirs exist in every part of the country. In urban areas, jazz and rock bars are popular. In Tallinn, Tartu, and Pärnu, bars and clubs are packed every Friday and Saturday night with people enjoying local rhythm and blues, rock, and jazz bands. Pärnu in particular is filled with music in the summer because of the influx of tourists and music events hosted by resorts. Young people also go to clubs and discos in the larger cities. Classical, opera, and choral works are well attended; concerts are held at the Estonia Concert Hall in Tallinn three times a week.

As in most other countries, people in Estonia like to watch movies. American and European documentaries and other films are shown with Estonian subtitles.

Locals such as this man enjoy fishing at frozen Lake Pühajärv during the winter season.

RURAL PURSUITS

In Estonia attachment to the land is strong. Favorite summer pastimes are walking and picking berries and mushrooms in the woods and forests. Camping on the coast, in the parks, or in the countryside is popular. Estonia has many campsites in the quiet rural areas. Estonia's lakes are sites for relaxation, and swimming is popular in summer. Some lakes, such as Pühajärv near Otepää, also have beaches. Pühajärv has a captivating, mystical atmosphere and was blessed by the Dalai Lama when he visited Tartu in 1992. Fishing is also a popular summer pursuit. In winter, people fish by cutting holes in the ice on the lakes.

Children and adults alike enjoy sledding down the soft winter snow.

Winter pastimes include ice-skating and tobogganing. Estonia's flat landscape and extensive winter snowfall make cross-country skiing a popular pursuit as well. The Otepää highlands receive more snow than any other part of the country. The town of Otepää is Estonia's winter sports center—there is downhill skiing, ski jumping, and numerous cross-country routes for enthusiasts. Each February about 12,000 Estonians and foreigners brave the freezing weather to participate in the Tartu Ski Marathon, a cross-country skiing race.

VACATIONS

Most urban Estonians take their summer vacation in the country, usually going to the national parks, islands, or picturesque regions in the south. The woods, islands, and lakes still offer a pristine freshness not found in many other parts of Europe. The low population density and undeveloped infrastructure mean buildings and fences rarely block a path or a view, giving the land an inviting openness. Pärnu is the most popular city destination.

Following the economic success since independence, more Estonians are taking vacations abroad. Finland and Sweden are by far the most popular foreign destinations, and they are quickly and easily reached by passenger ferry from Tallinn. Estonians also travel overland to Russia, Lithuania, Germany, and Latvia; some go as far afield as France, Spain, Italy, Britain, and the Netherlands. Flying long distance is still a luxury for Estonians, and few people travel as far as North America.

RESORTS AND SPAS

Estonia is blessed with many health resorts, ranging from sanatoriums and spa towns to lakeside camps and curative mud baths. The sanatorium in Kuressaare on Saaremaa has specialized in baths of curative sea mud since 1876. The mud gives off a terrible smell, and only the most dedicated mud bathers endure the treatment.

Pärnu is famous for its promenade and beaches. The Baltic Sea's shallow waters make bathing both warm and safe in summer months. In winter the water is ice-cold, and few people dare to swim.

A sanatorium health spa in Pärnu.

NATURE'S DOCTOR

Saunas are a fundamental aspect of Estonian rural life and a pastime Estonia has in common with Scandinavian countries (the word sauna was borrowed into English from Finnish, where the word is the same as in Estonian). In the past, peasants took saunas to treat illnesses rather than incurring the expense of calling a doctor. A basic sauna consists of a wooden room with benches and a hot stove, usually surrounded by bricks or stones, on which you toss water to produce clouds of steam. The steam helps open the bathers' pores and provides relaxation and a welcome relief from the extreme cold in winter. Saunas are said to be good for the lungs. Bathers often lightly brush their bodies with bunches of birch twigs, an action that increases perspiration and tingles the nerve ends. Taking a sauna is considered a highly personal experience, and an invitation to share a sauna is a friendly and hospitable gesture.

Haapsalu was developed as a spa town in the 19th century, though its curative mud is now considered of poor quality. A railroad was built to provide access to the town for the Russian aristocracy, and a long covered platform shelters visitors from the rain. Tchaikovsky, the famous Russian composer, often visited Haapsalu in summer, where he is said to have borrowed a motif from an Estonian folk song when composing his Sixth Symphony. The forested park and the beach of Paralepa near Haapsalu are popular with vacationers.

A facial treatment at the Lauaasmaa Spa.

SPORTS

Estonia has been internationally successful in many sports, especially wrestling. From 1920 to 1993, Estonians won more than 300 gold medals in Olympic, European, and world championships—an impressive tally for one of Europe's smallest nations.

It is commonly remarked that sports in Estonia began with Georg Lurich, who won the Greco—Roman world wrestling championship in 1901. Lurich, a remarkable athlete, was also a champion weightlifter. The first Estonian to win an Olympic medal was the wrestler Martin Klein, in 1912. In 1923 the Estonian Olympic Committee was created in the newly independent country, and Estonia achieved international success in track-and-field events. Estonia's international marksmen team won competitions in the 1920s and 1930s, including the Copa Argentina three times (1935, 1937, and 1939).

From 1945 until 1991, Estonian athletes represented the USSR in sporting competitions. Jaan Talts, a champion weightlifter, was three times world champion and four times European champion in the 1960s and 1970s. Heino Lipp was a decathlon champion in the postwar years, though the Soviet authorities never allowed him to compete in the Olympic Games because of his public disavowal of Communism. In 1989, however, Estonian sports were reorganized and the national Olympic committee restored. Lipp attended the 1992 Olympic Games and carried the Estonian flag in Estonia's first Olympic competition after the breakup of the USSR.

Mass cycle races, such as this one in Tartu, are very popular with Estonians.

In cycling, Aavo Pikkuus won the Soviet road racing championship in 1975 and 1976, while Erika Salumäe—Estonia's most accomplished female cyclist—won an Olympic gold medal as part of the Soviet sprinting team in 1988. Four years later, she won another gold medal at the Barcelona Olympics, competing this time under the Estonian flag. Decathlete Erki Nool won an Olympic gold in 2000, while cross-country skier Andrus Veerpalu gained a gold and a silver medal at the 2002 Olympics. At the 2008 Olympics, Gerd Kanter won a gold medal in the men's discus throw.

The former USSR was renowned for producing top chess players. Emerging in the 1930s, Estonian Paul Keres was one of the best chess players in the world for 40 years. Three times Soviet chess champion, Keres played in 66 international tournaments, winning seven Chess Olympiad gold medals.

Basketball is the most popular sport in Estonia today. Its roots in the country go back to the 1930s, when neighboring countries Latvia and Lithuania won the European championships, and the sport grew in popularity during the Soviet period. Today Tallinn's basketball teams, which include Baltika Tallinn, BC Tallinn, and BC Kalev Tallinn, are among the best in Europe. Ice hockey and soccer are also popular sports.

SAILING

In a country with a long coastline and numerous islands, sailing is a natural pastime. The Baltic Sea is very shallow and freezes easily, so sailing is a summer activity. Estonia's waters are considered the best in the region for sailing, and the Pirita Olympic Sports Center is one of the best equipped. The center was built for the 1980 Olympic Games in Moscow, during which all the sailing events were held in Tallinn. Haapsalu is one of the few other places in Estonia to have a yacht club, which opened in 1992. It successfully hosted the World Ice Yachting Championship in 1991. There are many minor marinas in Estonia, and yachts, dinghies, and sailboats bob on the waters of fishing ports throughout the country.

A marina in the Pirita River. Sailing on the rivers is safer than sailing in the strait between the west coast and the islands of Hiiumaa, Vormsi, and Muhu. The Muhu Channel is marked throughout with buoys, and only the most skillful sailors navigate it without problems.

FESTIVALS

Huge crowds at the Estonian Song
and Dance Festival in Tallinn.

ESTONIA IS HOME TO MANY festivals and cultural events, especially during the summer months. Tallinn in particular comes alive from May to September. Many regions and towns have their own local celebrations when people dress in traditional clothes. On festival days it is traditional to brew and drink beer, a custom Estonians have had no problem maintaining over the centuries.

Song festivals have long held political significance in Estonia. The first song festival was in 1869 during the country's national and cultural reawakening. Under Soviet rule, the song festivals became one of the few legal means for Estonians to celebrate their identity and express national pride. It was at the Baltica folk festival in 1988 that the national flags of the former Baltic republics were first publicly displayed without the offenders being arrested. These displays of nationalism were the beginning of the movement later dubbed the Singing Revolution.

A traditionally dressed musician.

January 1	*New Year's Day*
February 24	*Independence Day (1918)*
March/April	*Good Friday*
May 1	*May Day*
June 23	*Victory Day, marking the battle of Võnnu (1919)*
June 24	*Saint John's Day/Midsummer Day*
August 20	*Day of Restoration of Independence (1991)*
December 25 and 26	*Christmas*

MUSIC FESTIVALS

Throughout the Baltic countries song and dance festivals are held every summer. These events attract many visitors, especially Baltic people living abroad. The amphitheater of Tallinn's Song Celebration Grounds can hold up to 30,000 singers and has space for an audience of more than 150,000. Such is the popularity of singing festivals that there is rarely an empty seat.

The All-Estonian Song Festival takes place every five years in July. This weekend event is the country's oldest song festival. Remarkably, 500,000 people attended the 1990 festival, almost half of the ethnic Estonian population. It was an extremely emotional event that climaxed with a mass choir of 30,000 singers singing Estonian national songs. The most recent All-Estonian Song Festival was held in 2009.

Rock Summer is the Baltic's biggest rock music festival. For three days in July, well-known international and local acts play to a packed stadium. Rock Summer is gaining international recognition and has been broadcast on British television and MTV Europe.

Estonia hosts many other music festivals in the spring and summer months, including Jazzkaar, an internationally renowned jazz festival held every April in Tallinn; Muhu Future Music Festival, showcasing experimental popular, classical, and jazz music on the island of Muhu in early July; and the Blues Festival, held in August in Haapsalu.

CALENDER OF FESTIVALS

April	*Jazzkaar: international jazz festival in Tallinn*
May	*International Puppet Festival: held in Viljandi's puppet theater*
May	*International Dance Festival: contemporary dance from throughout Europe in Tartu*
June	*Pühajärv Beach Party: pop festival with live bands and DJs*
June 23	*Midsummer (Jaanipäev). The shortest night of the year features bonfires at hundreds of public and private celebrations*
Late June	*Hansa Days: medieval-style fair with street performances and music in Tartu*
June through August	*Summer Music Festival: classical, popular, and jazz concerts in various venues in Tartu*
July	*Beer Summer: gathering in Tallinn to taste local and international brews*
July	*Rock Summer: the Baltic region's biggest three-day international rock music festival, held in the Tallinn Song Celebration Grounds*
July	*Viljandi Folk Music Festival: the most widely attended world-music festival in the Baltic*
August	*Days of the Seto Kingdom: folk festival in Obinitsa celebrating the culture of the Seto people*
December	*Dark Nights Film Festival: Tallinn's annual art-house film festival*

Smaller, local song festivals are held throughout the country. Since 1984, Estonia has hosted an International Organ Music Festival, usually held in early August, when some of the world's leading organists perform in Tallinn's beautiful, historic churches. The festival often moves around the country as well, playing in various locations.

FOLK FESTIVALS

By far the most important folk festival in the Baltic is the Baltica festival, held annually in one of the three Baltic countries each summer. The festival celebrates the folklore and culture of small, little-known ethnic groups throughout Europe. Folk dancers and singers from Estonia, Lithuania, and Latvia gather to celebrate the weeklong festival with dancing, singing, parades, and exhibitions.

There are numerous other folk festivals; for example, the Viljandi Folk Music Festival draws international fans and performers of world music. Every June, Old Tallinn Days celebrates traditional Estonian culture with much jollity, music, and dancing through the streets of the capital's Old Town. In early September, Tallinn also hosts Lillepidu, an international flower festival that attracts thousands of spectators.

Women dressed in the brightest colors at a folk festival.

Baltica is one of the most colorful events on the Baltic folk calendar, especially because of the many unusual and picturesque folk costumes on display.

MIDSUMMER

The holidays of Võidupüha, or Victory Day, and Jaanipäev, or Saint John's Day, on June 23 and 24 combine the age-old pagan midsummer festival with the more modern, nationalistic celebration of the battle of Võnnu, during which, in 1919, the Estonian army thwarted the Baltic German army's attempt to regain control of Estonia.

As can be expected from a region where summers are short and winters are long, dark, and cold, Midsummer Day—as Saint John's Day is also called— has been a major celebration since pagan times and is deeply rooted in Estonian peasant culture. Jaanipäev marks the longest day of the year, when the evening twilight and emerging dawn seem to become one. At this time of year the light never fully fades. On the night of June 23 and the morning of June 24, villagers gather around a bonfire to sing, dance, and make merry.

In the past, the evening of Midsummer Day was considered a time of sorcery and magic. Purifying bonfires were lit to fend off evil spirits, and people would leap over them, as superstition had it that a successful clearance indicated a successful year ahead. Võidupüha and Jaanipäev usually merge into one long holiday.

Folk instruments, along with folk dress, are featured in Estonian festivals. In Estonia most of the the traditional instruments are also common throughout the rest of northern and eastern Europe: the zither, the whistle, the accordion, the flute, the goat's horn, and the violin. The guitar is also widely played. The one instrument unique to the Baltic lands is the kannel.

The kannel is a kind of zither that has between five and 12 iron or natural-fiber strings pulled taut over a board. This instrument has been used in the region for at least 3,000 years. The name derives from a proto-Baltic word meaning "the singing tree." The kannel is considered sacred, and according to folklore, the tree from which the instrument is to be made must be cut when someone has died but is not yet buried. The fine, deeply affecting tones of the instrument have come to symbolize Estonia's traditional national music. Larger, more elaborate versions of the kannel became widespread in the 19th century, and in the Soviet period, a many-stringed version of the instrument was developed to play Soviet-approved folk music.

Since the 1980s, renewed interest in traditional music has led to a revival of the original kannel, plus an interest in other traditional instruments similar to the jaw harp, the bagpipe, the reed, whistles, clappers, and rattles. Many of the simpler traditional instruments are made by the players themselves, while the more sophisticated instruments, such as the bagpipe or the kannel, are made by a few trained masters.

INDEPENDENCE DAY

Estonians celebrate their independence on February 24, the day the Republic of Estonia was first declared in 1918. The declaration was followed by a two-year war of independence, during which the fledgling Estonian army held off attacks by the Russian army and the Baltic German forces. The Tartu Peace Treaty of 1920 secured Estonia's borders for the first time in the country's history. Estonians take great pride in marking their hard-won independence, which serves as a permanent reminder of the Soviet Union's illegal 50-year occupation. People celebrate by gathering to eat and drink, while the Estonian flag hangs from almost every building as an expression of national pride. The day is officially marked with the raising of the national flag at dawn from the tallest tower in Tallinn Old Town.

RELIGIOUS HOLIDAYS

The vast majority of ethnic Estonians are nominally Lutheran in faith. Although they celebrate the major festivals of Christmas and Easter, the Christian holidays do not create the kind of excitement or activity associated with the song festivals.

A beautifully lit Christmas tree in a market in Estonia.

Christmas is celebrated in much the same way as in other northern European countries. On Christmas Eve, most Estonians celebrate by having a meal, visiting family and friends, and relaxing in their homes. Often the close proximity of the New Year provides them with an excuse to have a long midwinter break. Shrove Tuesday, during the seventh week before Easter, is usually observed in February. Children often go tobogganing on this day; it is believed that a long sleigh slide indicates a fruitful summer harvest. At Easter time, people dye eggs and give eggs as presents. Traditionally eggs were dyed using onion skins or leaves from birch switches. Shops, offices, and businesses are usually closed from the Thursday before Good Friday until the Tuesday after Easter Monday.

FOOD

A waitress from the Olde Hansa Restaurant in Tallinn shows off the delicious Estonian fare.

CHAPTER 13

ESTONIAN COOKING IS WHOLESOME fare based on a traditional, rural diet with few frills and no spices. The main ingredients of the Estonian diet are meat (especially pork), bread, fruit, root vegetables, and varieties of mushrooms, berries, and nuts in summer.

Fresh milk is also a dominant ingredient, as is cheese, especially for making sauces. Estonians tend to bake, roast, or boil their food; very little traditional Baltic food is fried.

Vegetable store vendors at Balti Jaam Station Market in Tallinn.

Bread made from refined white flour is traditionally eaten only on special occasions. The ultimate white bread is *kringel*, a large, braided loaf filled with nuts and raisins and prepared in the shape of a pretzel. *Kringel* is usually served on birthdays and holidays.

Rustic rye bread and accompanying soup.

A typical breakfast in Estonia might include any or all of the following: porridge, cottage cheese, bread with salted fish, and fried or hard-boiled eggs with smoked ham, all washed down with plenty of coffee or sometimes tea. Lunch is likely to consist of three courses: a substantial first course of cold dishes followed by roast pork with potatoes and other vegetables and finished off with a mousse, a sweet bread soup, or baked apples, depending on the season. Traditionally supper is a lighter meal than lunch, consisting of roast meats or pickled fish. It is the custom for people to say "*Head isu!*" (HEH-uht-EE-soo), which roughly translates as "Enjoy your meal," before commencing a meal.

BREAD

Leib (LAY-p), or bread, is the essential staple of the Estonian diet and accompanies every meal. Because of food shortages in the past, bread has attained an almost religious significance among Estonians. Consequently bread is never thrown away but often reappears in a different guise, such as in *leiva supp* (LAY-vuh soop), a sweet, black-colored, bread soup.

Most Estonian bread is of the dark brown, wholemeal variety. Bread made from barley is a speciality and is often sweetened with honey. *Rukkileib* (RUK-kee-lay-p), rye bread enhanced with molasses, is also popular and a perfect accompaniment for Estonia's mild cheeses and spicy beer.

THE COLD TABLE

The first course in most Estonian meals is a selection of cold dishes. Traditionally two-thirds of the meal consisted of cold dishes; as in Sweden and Russia, it is still considered the best way of showing off local produce. Often these cold dishes are as substantial as the main course. *Rosolje* (roh-SOHL-yuh), a delicious salad based on beets, meat, and herring, is the signature dish of Estonian cuisine. It is often served as a first course or a luncheon dish on a warm summer day. Small pies called *pirukas* (PI-ru-kuhs), filled with meat, carrots, and cabbage, are also served.

Fish—especially herring—is a part of the cold table. Estonia is famous throughout the region for its sprats (canned fish similar to sardines), which have been a local favorite since the Middle Ages.

MEAT AND POTATOES

Estonian food is very much of the "meat and potatoes" variety, covered in a rich gravy. Potatoes were introduced in the 18th century and have been a mainstay of the Estonian diet ever since. Pork is the most important meat

Smoked meats, such as goose and ham, are popular traditional dishes in the eastern Baltic, dating from a time when the lack of refrigeration made preserving meat a necessity.

Pirukas are one of the most popular Estonian cold dishes.

and is eaten in various forms: roasted, cured as bacon or ham, or in pies, sausage, and black pudding (also known as blood sausage). Sauerkraut (cabbage fermented in brine) is often served with pork.

SOUPS AND DESSERTS

Estonia's soups are generally bland, creamy dishes made chiefly from milk and vegetables, or perhaps with yogurt and dill cucumber. Unusually, many soups are eaten as desserts. *Kissell* (kee-SELL), a clear, sweet soup, is made from garden berries and red currants and served with white bread. Raspberry soup—liquidized raspberries boiled and whisked into a soup, then served with a dash of lemon and sour cream—is delicious, and many restaurants in Tallinn consider it their speciality.

Berries, apples, and rhubarbs appear in various guises—including stewed or baked in a pie. Baked apple is usually served with milk and sugar. *Mannapuder* (MAH-nah-pood-ah) is a kind of semolina milk pudding, similar to American cream of wheat, that can be found throughout Estonia. Torten, a favorite party dessert, came to Estonia as a legacy of the Baltic barons. Fluffy, plate-size pancakes, usually filled with raspberries or blueberries, are also popular. Sweet whipped cream is often added to cakes and pies.

This Swedish baked apple pudding is a favorite among many Estonians.

Food from the former Soviet republics in the Caucasus is very popular, especially *šašlõkk* kebab and grilled lamb.

THIRST QUENCHERS

Traditional drinks include ales and meads, teas brewed from plants found in the garden or the woods, and milk. Juices and cordials made from local summer fruit such as gooseberries, rhubarbs, and junipers have been enjoyed in the region for centuries. A preference for coffee over tea distinguishes the Baltic peoples from their Slavic neighbors, and coffeehouses and cafés are numerous throughout Estonia's cities and towns.

Lager and ale of the dark variety found in other parts of northern Europe have traditionally been brewed in Estonia. Saare beer, brewed on the island of Saaremaa, is considered one of Estonia's best traditional beers, while Saku Reval Luksus is a popular, Western-style, bottled beer. Kali (also called Kvass) is a rye-based soft drink of Russian origin.

Popular spirits include cognac, vodka, and the locally produced Vana Tallinn liqueur. For many years people in the Baltic countries have made their own moonshine vodka from rye.

EATING OUT

Since independence, the choice of both Estonian and international cuisines available in Estonia's towns and cities has dramatically improved. Tallinn in particular offers Chinese, Korean, Italian, Mexican, Middle Eastern, and Indian food, as well as many restaurants serving hearty, traditional Estonian cuisine. Local fast-food chains offering pizza, pasta, salads, and burgers can be found in every part of the country, as can the better-known international burger chains. After work, Estonia's cafés are swamped by people seeking good coffee and tasty pastries. Tallinn's many dark, stuffy cellar bars are great on atmosphere but badly ventilated, chiefly as a result of the traditional insulation against the harsh winter.

Various types of locally brewed Estonian beers.

Garden produce plays a vital part in Estonian cuisine. In rural areas, people grow tomatoes, peas, cucumbers, beets, rutabagas, zucchinis, turnips, potatoes, cabbages, and rhubarbs. Apple and plum trees are also numerous. From beyond the garden, wild nuts, berries, and mushrooms have been gathered for centuries from the surrounding woods and fields.

VAARIKA SUP (RASPBERRY SOUP)

4 servings

1 ½ pounds (700 g) raspberries

6 ounces (170 g) red currants

¾ pint (450 ml) water

1 tablespoon (15 ml) cornstarch

Juice and rind of ½ lemon

4—5 ounces (110—140 g) light brown sugar

½ teaspoon (2.5 ml) cinnamon

9-10 fluid ounces (275 ml) whipping cream

¼ pint (150 ml) sour cream

Put aside a large handful of raspberries for garnish. Place the remaining raspberries and all the red currants in a food processor, and mix until the berries are liquid.

Place a fine sieve over a stainless-steel saucepan. Press the pureed fruit so that the seeds are removed, stirring through the sieve in batches until all the liquid has passed into the saucepan.

Add the water to the strained fruit. Place over high heat and bring to a boil, then lower the heat, and simmer for 15 minutes.

In a small bowl, mix the cornstarch with a little water. Whisk into the soup, turn up the heat, and continue whisking as the soup begins to boil and thicken. Lower the heat and mix in the lemon juice and rind, sugar, and cinnamon.

Remove from the heat, allow to cool, then chill for several hours.

Before serving, stir in the whipping cream and the sour cream. Spoon into individual soup bowls, and garnish each with some of the reserved berries.

PEEDI-KARTULISALAT (BEET AND POTATO SALAD)

4 servings

2 boiled beets, peeled

6 boiled potatoes, peeled

1 large salad onion

sour cream

salt

fresh chives, finely chopped

Chop the beets and the potatoes into small cubes. Finely slice the onion. Mix the beets, potatoes, and onion in a bowl. Add enough sour cream to bind everything together. Season with salt. Let the flavors infuse for 30 minutes in a fridge. Sprinkle plenty of chopped chives on top and serve.

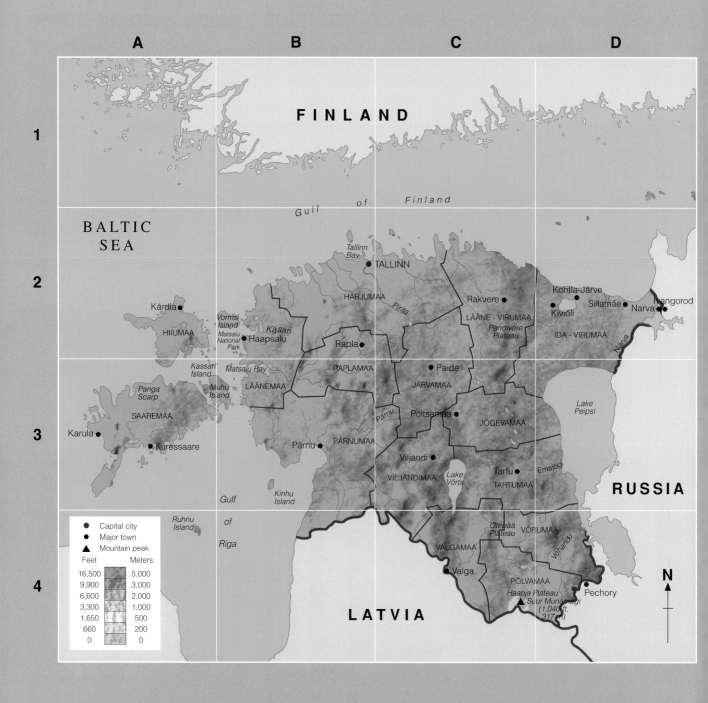

A   **B**   **C**   **D**

FINLAND

1

BALTIC
SEA

Gulf   of   Finland

*Tallinn
Bay*
● TALLINN

2

Kärdla ●

HARJUMAA

Pirita

Rakvere ●

Kohtla-Järve ●

Ivangorod ●

*Vormsi
Island*
HIIUMAA

Kasari
*Matsalu
National
Park*
Haapsalu ●

LÄÄNE - VIRUMAA

*Pandivere
Plateau*

Sillamäe ●

Narva ●

Kiviõli ●

IDA - VIRUMAA

Narva

Rapla ●

*Kassari
Island*

Matsalu Bay

RAPLAMAA

Paide ●

JÄRVAMAA

*Lake
Peipsi*

*Panga
Scarp*

*Muhu
Island*

LÄÄNEMAA

3

SAAREMAA

Karula ●

Kuressaare ●

Pärnu

Põltsamaa ●

JÕGEVAMAA

Pärnu ●

PÄRNUMAA

Viljandi ●

Tartu ●

Emajõgi

RUSSIA

VILJANDIMAA

*Lake
Võrts*

TARTUMAA

*Kinhu
Island*

Gulf

*Otepää
Plateau*

VÕRUMAA

*Ruhnu
Island*

of

VALGAMAA

Võhardu

Riga

Valga ●

PÕLVAMAA

Pechory ●

4

Haanja Plateau
▲ *Suur Munamägi*
*(1,040 ft.
317 m)*

LATVIA

● Capital city
● Major town
▲ Mountain peak

Feet	Meters
16,500	5,000
9,900	3,000
6,600	2,000
3,300	1,000
1,650	500
660	200
0	0

N

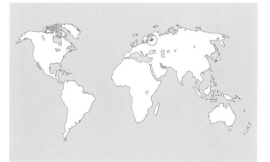

ECONOMIC ESTONIA

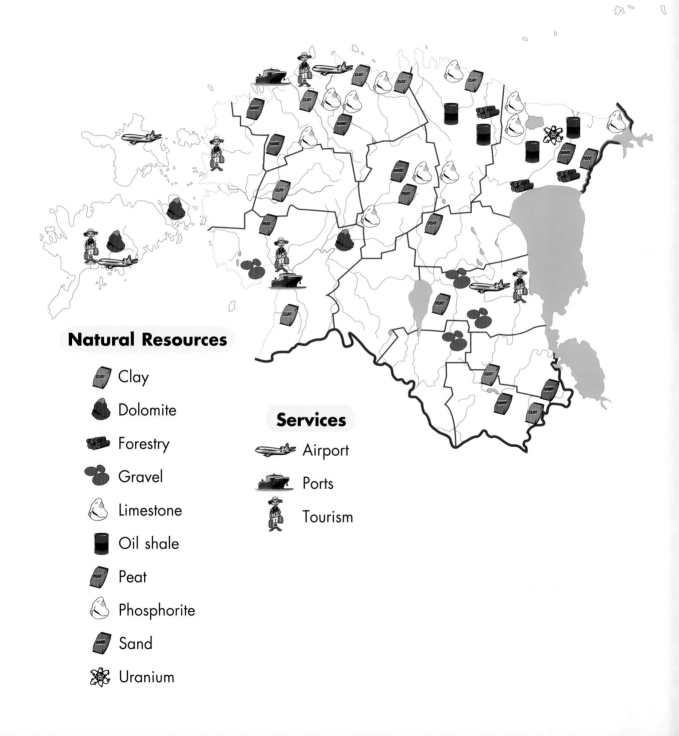

Natural Resources

- Clay
- Dolomite
- Forestry
- Gravel
- Limestone
- Oil shale
- Peat
- Phosphorite
- Sand
- Uranium

Services

- Airport
- Ports
- Tourism

ABOUT THE ECONOMY

OVERVIEW

Estonia has a modern market-based economy and one of the highest per-capita (per-person) income levels in Eastern Europe. Since independence, Estonia's various governments have put into practice free-market, probusiness policies and reforms. Estonia became a member of the EU in 2004. During the subsequent four years, the economy had a high growth rate, averaging 8 percent per year. Estonia has strong trade ties with Finland, Sweden, and Germany, with the electronics and telecommunications industries a source of export and import business. However, rapid growth brought high inflation and weakened the country's currency. The government wants to join the euro, but no date has been set. Similar to those of many other countries, Estonia's economy slowed and fell into recession in mid-2008, with the decline continuing into 2009.

GROSS DOMESTIC PRODUCT (GDP)

$25.21 billion (2008 est.)

GDP PER CAPITA

$21,900 (2008 est.)

CURRENCY

Estonian kroon (EEK)
$1 = 12.1 EEK (March 2009)

LABOR FORCE

686,000 (2008 est.)

LABOR FORCE BY TYPE OF JOB

agriculture: 5.3 percent
industry: 34 percent
services: 60.7 percent (2005)

UNEMPLOYMENT RATE

5.1 percent (2008 est.)

NATURAL RESOURCES

Oil shale, peat, phosphorite, clay, limestone, sand, dolomite, arable land, sea mud

MAIN INDUSTRIES

Engineering, electronics, wood and wood products, textiles, information technology, telecommunications

MAIN EXPORTS

Machinery and equipment, 33 percent; wood and paper, 15 percent; textiles, 14 percent; food products, 8 percent; furniture, 7 percent

MAIN IMPORTS

Machinery and equipment, 33.5 percent; chemical products, 11.6 percent; textiles, 10.3 percent; food products, 9.4 percent; transportation equipment, 8.9 percent

CULTURAL ESTONIA

Tallinn Old Town
Tallinn Old Town is listed as a UNESCO World Heritage site for its well-preserved medieval architecture—such as the Crusader-built Toompea Castle, the 15th-century House of the Great Guild, and Town Hall Square.

Kumu Art Museum, Tallinn
Opened in 2006, the Kumu Art Museum is the largest art museum in the Baltic region and one of the largest art museums in northern Europe. The architecturally impressive building is located on 9.9 acres (4 ha) in Tallinn, on the limestone bank of Lasnamägi next to Kadriorg Park, and displays Estonian art from the 18th century to the present.

Lahemaa National Park
Situated on a long stretch of indented coastline to the east of Tallinn, the park is marked by four distinctive peninsulas protruding into the Gulf of Finland. Lahemaa has some of the most beautiful and varied landscape in the country, with deserted beaches, reedbeds, and lush forests home to most species of wildlife native to Estonia.

Song Bowl
Estonia's premier festival arena is located outside of Narva. Built in the 1960s, it has been the main venue for Estonia's biannual song festival ever since. The Song Bowl can hold up to 15,000 singers on the stage alone and an additional 30,000 performers on the platform in front of the stage.

Toompea Castle
Built in the 13th century at the top of a limestone outcrop that looms over Tallinn's Old Town, this Livonian Order fortress was the nerve center of Christian medieval Tallinn and includes the imposing Pikk Hermann (Tall Hermann), a 164-foot (50-m) tower dating from 1371.

Vilsandi National Park
Located off the western shore of Saaremaa Island, this national reserve's offshore islets and reedbeds are home to a multitude of migratory birds.

Pärnu
Pärnu is home to one of Esonia's most impressive, unspoilt sandy beaches, where beautiful sunsets can be seen from a recently constructed boardwalk along the seafront. The seaside town is also an internationally recognized health resort, with curative mud baths and other health therapies.

Tartu University
The main, architecturally impressive 17th-century structure of what many Estonians consider the national university includes four museums and a botanical garden. Dozens of other historic buildings spread around Tartu belong to the university as well.

Setumaa
Setumaa is home to Estonia's most distinctive minority. The Setos retain their own dialect and culture, with artistic traditions that have died out elsewhere.

Piusa Sand Caves
North of the town of Obinitsa, in the southeast corner of Estonia, the Piusa Sand Caves are a series of sandstone chambers excavated over many decades by the glassmaking industry. The caves have since become an important habitat for bats and were designated a protected nature reserve in 1999.

OFFICIAL NAME
Eesti Vabariik (Republic of Estonia)

LAND AREA
17,462 square miles (45,226 sq km)

CAPITAL
Tallinn

MAJOR CITIES
Tartu, Narva, Kohtla-Järve, Pärnu

COUNTIES (*Maakonnad*)
Harjumaa, Lääne-Virumaa, Ida-Virumaa, Järvamaa, Jõgevamaa, Viljandimaa, Tartumaa, Põlvamaa, Võrumaa, Valgamaa, Pärnumaa, Läänemaa, Raplamaa, Saaremaa, Hiiumaa

MAJOR RIVERS
Emajõgi, Pärnu, Narva

MAJOR LAKES
Peipsi, Võrtsjärv

HIGHEST POINT
Suur Manamägi (1,040 feet/317 m)

POPULATION
1,299,371 (July 2009 est.)

LIFE EXPECTANCY
total population: 72.56 years
male: 67.16 years
female: 78.3 years (2008 est.)

BIRTHRATE
1.42 children born per female (2008 est.)

ETHNIC GROUPS
Estonian, 68.6 percent; Russian, 24.9 percent; Ukrainian, 2.1 percent; Belarusian, 1.2 percent; Finnish, 0.8 percent; other, 2.4 percent (2000 census)

RELIGION
Lutheran, 13.6 percent; Orthodox, 12.8 percent; other Christian (including Methodist, Seventh-day Adventist, Roman Catholic, Pentecostal), 1.4 percent; unaffiliated, 34.1 percent; other and unspecified, 32 percent; none, 6.1 percent

LANGUAGES
Estonian (official), 67.3 percent; Russian, 29.7 percent; other, 2.3 percent; unknown, 0.7 percent (2000 census)

NATIONAL HOLIDAY
Independence Day, February 24

TIME LINE

IN ESTONIA	IN THE WORLD
A.D. 800–1100 Viking trade routes cross Estonia.	
1219 The Danes conquer northern Estonia.	**1206–1368** Genghis Khan unifies the Mongols and starts conquest of the world. At its height, the Mongol Empire under Kublai Khan stretches from China to Persia and parts of Europe and Russia.
1227 German crusaders from Riga conquer and Christianize southern Estonia.	
1346 The Danes sell northern Estonia to the German Livonian Order.	
1525 The first Estonian-language book is published.	
1561 Sweden conquers Estonia.	
1632 Tartu University is founded.	
1710 Russia conquers Estonia in the Great Northern War (1700–21).	
1718–36 Russian czar Peter the Great constructs the baroque peach-and-white Kadriorg Palace.	**1776** U.S. Declaration of Independence
1816 Serfdom is abolished in Estonia.	**1789–99** The French Revolution
1870 The Saint Petersburg-Tallinn railway is completed.	
1918 Independence proclaimed after German occupation and the collapse of imperial Russia at the end of World War I.	**1914** World War I begins.
1920 Peace treaty signed with Soviet Russia.	
1934 Prime Minister Konstantin Päts leads bloodless coup and establishes authoritarian rule.	
1940 Estonia is incorporated into the Soviet Union.	**1939** World War II begins.
1941 Nazi Germany occupies Estonia.	
1944 The German army retreats and Estonia is again occupied by the Soviet Union.	**1945** The United States drops atomic bombs on Hiroshima and Nagasaki. World War II ends.

IN ESTONIA	IN THE WORLD
1988	
Popular Front campaigns for democracy emerge amidst the Singing Revolution.	
1991	
Communist rule collapses, and the Soviet government recognizes the independence of the Baltic republics.	
1992	
Lennart Meri becomes Estonia's first postindependence president.	**1997** Hong Kong is returned to China.
2001	**2001**
Former Communist Party leader Arnold Rüütel is elected president.	Terrorists crash planes into New York, Washington D.C., and Pennsylvania.
2002	
Mart Laar resigns as prime minister, Siim Kallas becomes prime minister in a new coalition government.	
2003	**2003**
Following elections, President Rüütel invites Res Publica leader Juhan Parts to be prime minister in coalition government with Reform Party and People's Union. In a referendum, Estonians vote overwhelmingly to join the EU.	War in Iraq begins.
2004	
Estonia is admitted to the North Atlantic Treaty Organization (NATO).	
2005	
The Reform Party's Andrus Ansip is confirmed as prime minister.	
2006	
Toomas Hendrik Ilves is elected president.	
2007	
Estonia becomes the first country to allow Internet voting for national elections. The Reform Party wins by a narrow margin.	
2008	
Estonia goes into recession. Government budgets are cut. Unemployment rises. In a unique democratic experiment, the Estonian government sets up 410 internet sites across Estonia for citizens to share their ideas on how to deal with the economic crisis.	

GLOSSARY

Bolsheviks
Russian Communists.

glasnost
Russian for "openness"; a policy initiated by Mikhail Gorbachev of the Soviet Union.

head isu (HEH-uht-EE-soo)
The customary toast before commencing a meal, meaning "enjoy your meal."

Jaanipäev
Saint John's Day as well as the celebration of the age-old pagan festival of Midsummer Day.

kannel (KUHN-ehl)
A musical instrument, like a zither, first used 3,000 years ago, that has 5—12 iron or natural-fiber strings pulled taut over a board.

kissell (kee-SELL)
A clear, sweet soup made from garden berries and red currants.

leib (LAY-p)
Bread.

leiva supp (LAY-vuh soop)
A sweet, black bread soup, usually made from leftover bread, eaten as a dessert.

maakond (MAH-kont); plural, *maakonnad* (MAH-kon-ahd)
County; there are 15 *maakonnad* in Estonia.

maarahvas (MAH-rahh-vuhs)
"People of the land," the name Estonians called themselves before the mid-19th century.

mannapuder (MAH-nah-pood-ah)
A semolina milk pudding similar to cream of wheat.

perestroika
Russian word meaning "restructuring."

pirukas (PI-ru-kuhs)
Small pies filled with meat, carrots, and cabbage.

Riigikogu
The Estonian legislative assembly or parliament.

rosolje (roh-SOHL-yuh)
Salad whose main ingredients are beetroot, meat, and herring; considered typically Estonian.

rukkileib (RUK-kee-lay-p)
Rye bread enhanced with molasses, the favored accompaniment for Estonia's mild cheeses and spicy beer.

torte
A rich German cake.

Võidupüha
Victory Day, June 23, which is combined with Jaanipäev (see above) to make the midsummer holiday.

FOR FURTHER INFORMATION

BOOKS

Hiisjarv, Piret, and Ene Hiiepuu. *Looking at Estonia* (Looking at Europe). Minneapolis: Oliver Press, 2006.

Jarvis, Howard et al. *Estonia, Latvia, and Lithuania* (Eyewitness Travel Guide). London: DK Travel, 2009.

O'Connor, Kevin. *Culture and Customs of the Baltic States* (Culture and Customs of Europe). Westport, CT: Greenwood Press, 2006.

Otfinoski, Steven. *The Baltic Republics* (Nations in Transition). New York: Facts on File, 2004.

Thomson, Clare. *Estonia—Culture Smart!: a Quick Guide to Customs and Etiquette.* London: Kuperard, 2007.

Williams, Roger. *Baltic States Insight Guide.* Rev. ed. London: APA Publications, 2007.

FILMS

Arvo Pärt. *Te Deum/Silouans Song/Magnificat/Berliner Messe.* Ecm Records, 1993.

Heino Eller et al. *Music from Estonia.* Scottish National Orchestra, conductor Neeme Järvi, Chandos, 2005.

Veljo Tormis et al. *Vision of Estonia I.* Alba, 2003.

MUSIC

Heiki Ernits and Janno Põldma. *Lotte from Gadgetville.* Eesti Joonisfilm, 2006.

New Europe—Estonia. New Europe Music, 2007.

James Tusty and Maureen Castle Tusty. *The Singing Revolution.* Northern Lights, 2007.

BIBLIOGRAPHY

BOOKS

Clemens, Walter. *The Baltic Transformed*. Lanham, MD: Rowman & Littlefield, 2001.

Daitz, Mimi. *Ancient Song Recovered*. Hillsdale, NY: Pendragon Press, 2004.

Karner, Karin Annus. *Estonian Tastes and Traditions* (Hippocrene Cookbook Library). New York: Hippocrene Books, 2006.

Lieven, Anatol. *The Baltic Revolution: Estonia, Latvia, Lithuania, and the Path to Independence*. 4th ed. New Haven, CT: Yale University Press, 1994.

Page, Edita, ed. *The Baltic Quintet: Poetry from Estonia, Finland, Latvia, Lithuania, and Sweden*. Hamilton, Ontario: Wolsak and Wynn Publishers, 2008.

Raun, Toivo. *Estonia and the Estonians*. Stanford, CA: Hoover Institution Press, 2001.

Smith, David J. *Estonia: Independence and European Integration*. London: Routledge, 2002.

Williams, Nicola. *Estonia, Latvia, and Lithuania*. 4th ed. Oakland, CA: Lonely Planet, 2006.

WEBSITES

The Baltic Times, www.baltictimes.com

SmartEstonia.ee, www.smartestonia.ee

The State Portal, www.eesti/ee/eng

Statistics Estonia, www.stat.ee/?lang=en

Tallinn Tourism, www.tourism.tallinn.ee.

U.S. Department of State—Estonia, www.state.gov/p/eur/ci/en/.

Visit Estonia, www.visitestonia.com

INDEX

INDEX